readiscover...

BooksMusic**Film**Information**Computers**Local history
Family history**Newspapers**Magazines**Photocopying
Faxing**Games**Children's storytimes**Displays and events

Please return or renew this item by its due date to
avoid fines. You can renew by phone, online or in
person. You will need your library card and PIN.

24 hour renewals 0303 123 0035

Bletchley:	(01908) 372797
Kingston:	(01908) 282720
MK Central:	(01908) 254050
Newport Pagnell:	(01908) 610933
Olney:	(01234) 711474
Stony Stratford:	(01908) 562562
Westcroft:	(01908) 507874
Woburn Sands:	(01908) 582033
Wolverton:	(01908) 312812

www.milton-keynes.gov.uk/libraries

Milton Keynes Libraries

MILTON KEYNES
C O U N C I L

www.babaniboo

D1380332

79 602 390 9

Please Note

Although every care has been taken with the production of this book to ensure that all information is correct at the time of writing and that any projects, designs, modifications and/or programs, etc., contained herewith, operate in a correct and safe manner and also that any components specified are normally available in Great Britain, the Publishers and Author do not accept responsibility in any way for the failure (including fault in design) of any project, design, modification or program to work correctly or to cause damage to any equipment that it may be connected to or used in conjunction with, or in respect of any other damage or injury that may be so caused, nor do the Publishers accept responsibility in any way for the failure to obtain specified components.

Notice is also given that if equipment that is still under warranty is modified in any way or used or connected with home-built equipment then that warranty may be void.

© 2012 BERNARD BABANI (publishing) LTD

First Published – October 2012

British Library Cataloguing in Publication Data:

A catalogue record for this book is available from the British Library

ISBN 978-0-85934-734-1

Cover Design by Gregor Arthur

Printed and bound in Great Britain for Bernard Babani (publishing) Ltd

About this Book

Recent research in the United States and Great Britain has shown that social networking can have a positive effect on the health of older people. In later life we might see less of friends and family as they move away from home and our own mobility may decline. New technology has created "The Global Village", enabling people to keep in touch using just a computer and the Internet, wherever they are in the world. Now you can exchange news and photographs and see live video of the people you care about, without leaving your own home. So it's hardly surprising that keeping in touch in this way brings real health benefits.

The first part of the book shows how to get started with Facebook, the world's most popular social network, enabling you to build up a list of Facebook friends. By entering your personal profile you can make friends with other people having a similar background and interests and exchange news and information.

The book then describes Twitter, another extremely popular social network which allows you to quickly post off short, concise text messages (called "Tweets") for your followers to read and respond to. Followers may include your own friends and family. You may also choose to follow the Tweets of well-known people or contribute your views to popular causes and debates.

The last chapter looks at some other useful tools which help people to keep in touch. These include the blog, a sort of online diary in which you report regularly on situations as they develop. Both Skype and Windows Live Messenger allow you to make free telephone calls over the Internet and to use webcams to actually see people, live in real time. Outlook.com is a new e-mail service designed to replace Hotmail and integrate with Facebook, Twitter, Skype and the Skydrive "cloud" storage. Outlook.com is discussed in detail but as Hotmail is still very widely used, it is referred to in examples throughout this book.

N.B. Throughout this book, click or clicking refers to the left-hand mouse button unless otherwise specified.

About the Author

Jim Gatenby trained as a Chartered Mechanical Engineer and initially worked at Rolls-Royce Ltd using computers in the analysis of jet engine performance. He obtained a Master of Philosophy degree in Mathematical Education by research at Loughborough University of Technology and taught mathematics and computing in school for many years before becoming a full-time author. His most recent teaching posts included Head of Computer Studies and Information Technology Co-ordinator. The author has written over thirty books in the field of educational computing, including many of the titles in the highly successful 'Older Generation' series from Bernard Babani (publishing) Ltd.

Trademarks

Microsoft, Windows, Windows Live Messenger, Windows 7, Windows Live Photo Gallery, Internet Explorer, Skype, Word, Excel, Publisher, Paint, Outlook.com and Hotmail are either trademarks or registered trademarks of Microsoft Corporation. Firefox is a trademark of the Mozilla Foundation. Facebook is a registered trademark of Facebook, Inc. Twitter is a registered trademark of Twitter, Inc. Blogger is a trademark or registered trademark of Google, Inc.

All other brand and product names used in this book are recognized as trademarks or registered trademarks of their respective companies.

Acknowledgements

As usual I would like to thank my wife Jill for her continued support during the preparation of this book. Also Michael Babani for making this project possible.

Contents

6

More Facebook Activities

7

Putting Your Photos on Facebook

14

15

Getting Started With Facebook

What is Facebook?

This chapter gives an overview of Facebook, what you can do with it and how to get started. Later chapters give step-by-step instructions showing you how to use the main features.

Facebook is a Web site which allows anyone to create Web pages about themselves and these can be viewed on a computer anywhere in the world. All you need is a computer connected to the Internet, a Web browser such as Internet Explorer or Mozilla Firefox and a valid e-mail address. You also need to be at least 13 years of age. Once you've signed up for a Facebook account you can start exchanging information with people you have chosen to accept as *Facebook friends*. Facebook, together with competitors such as Twitter, are known as *social networking* Web sites. At the time of writing Facebook is the biggest with over a billion users around the world.

Signing up for a Facebook account is free — the company derives its income from advertisements. A sample Facebook page is shown below with some adverts on the lower right.

Am I Too Old to Use Facebook?

The answer to this frequently asked question is "Certainly not!" In 2010 Facebook had at least one prolific user of over 100 years of age, a lady with nearly 5000 Facebook friends. Admittedly Facebook had its roots among university students in the USA. It was launched in 2004 by Harvard student Mark Zuckerberg, who went on to become the world's youngest billionaire. However, with the rapid growth of the Internet, this form of electronic communication between friends rapidly expanded beyond the universities into the wider world. Facebook is now widely used by people of all ages and diverse backgrounds and is even the subject of a major film "The Social Network".

Recent years have seen Facebook become popular with millions of older people. This is not surprising since older people often want to keep in touch with friends and family who have moved away; it may be difficult or impossible for older people to travel to see children or friends in person. Facebook allows you to keep in touch electronically by exchanging your latest news, photographs, video clips and contact details, for example.

It's Easier Than You Think

Unfortunately many older people are mistakenly put off using computers, thinking they are too difficult to use and the exclusive preserve of youngsters. This is quite wrong — Facebook is easy for anyone to use and you don't need to be a young computer wizard or "geek" to enjoy it. This book takes you step-by-step through the stages of setting up your new Facebook account and using the main features.

If you are new to computing and need some help with the basic skills you may be interested in some of my other books from Bernard Babani (publishing) Ltd. These include "Basic Computing for the Older Generation" (ISBN 978-0-85934-731-0) and "An Introduction to the Internet for the Older Generation" (ISBN 978-0-85934-711-2).

What Can Facebook Be Used For?

Listed below are some of the many Facebook facilities:

- Creating an easily accessible network of contacts, collectively known as *friends* and also including family, work colleagues or perhaps customers of a business.

- Other people may send a request to become your friend and you can accept or reject them. You can invite people to be your friend and remove existing friends if you wish.

- Providing a personal *profile* or *timeline* which your friends can read at any time. This includes photos and up-to-date contact details, such as telephone number and e-mail address, enabling friends to stay in touch.

- The profile can include details of your education and career, allowing old friends and colleagues to contact you. Listing your interests, likes and dislikes may enable you to join a Facebook *group* for like-minded people.

- You can include as much or as little information as you like in your profile and this can be edited or deleted at any time. *Audience selectors* are used to control who sees what pieces of information, ranging from *public* (viewable by everyone) to the *friends only* setting.

- *Status updates* are text messages posted on your Facebook *Wall*, a page telling friends your news and this can include photos, video clips and links to Web sites.

- You can build up *photograph albums* on your Facebook page, easily accessible to all your friends.

- You can use Facebook to publicise future events or promote a business. A group of friends with a common interest can join an online discussion or a campaign.

- Facebook provides access to third-party software (known as *applications* or *apps*) to do specific tasks such as editing photographs or playing games.

Everything You Need

The only requirements to start using Facebook are:

- A computer with an Internet connection.
- A Web browser such as Internet Explorer or Mozilla Firefox.
- A valid e-mail address such as:

    johnsmith@live..co.uk.
- You must be at least 13 years of age.

The Computer

The work on Facebook in this book has been carried out using PC-type laptop and desktop computers running the Microsoft Windows 7 operating system, but any PC or Apple computer made in the last few years will be quite adequate.

A *laptop* computer or its small relative the *netbook* will give you the freedom to use Facebook on the move. Laptops typically have a screen size of approximately 15 inches, (measured diagonally), while the netbook screen is usually about 10 inches. The latest handheld *tablet computers* such as the iPad and the Samsung Galaxy are also suitable for running Facebook.

The Web Browser

Most computers use the Microsoft Internet Explorer *Web browser* to display Web pages such as Facebook, but you might equally use another browser such as the very popular Mozilla Firefox, downloadable for free from **www.mozilla.org**.

Launching Facebook

Open your Web browser such as Internet Explorer (top screenshot) or Mozilla Firefox and enter the Facebook address into the Address Bar at the top of the screen, as shown in the extracts below.

(In practice you only need to type **facebook.com**).

Signing Up

The Facebook sign-up page opens as shown below. Enter your first and last names, e-mail address and a new password for Facebook in the boxes shown on the right below. Then select your gender and date of birth from the drop-down menus. The date of birth is used to check you're at least 13 years of age. Later on your date of birth can be omitted from your profile page if you prefer that other people don't see it.

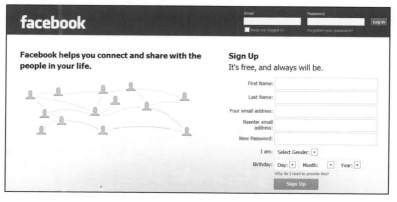

Existing users of Facebook also use the sign-up page every time they log in by entering their e-mail address and password as shown below and on the sign-up screen on the previous page.

At the bottom right of the sign-up page is a link (shown in blue under **Sign Up** below) allowing you to create a Facebook page to promote a celebrity, band or business. There is also an option to create a community page to gather support for a cause or topic close to your heart.

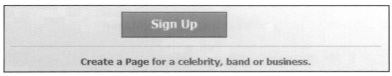

These alternative uses of Facebook are discussed later in this book; this chapter now continues with the signing-up process for the general Facebook individual user.

After completing the sign-up screen shown on page 5, new Facebook users click the **Sign Up** button and are presented with a CAPTCHA security check as shown below. Type the distorted words into the boxes below to prove that a human being is completing the form and not a fraudulent computer system.

After you click **Sign Up** the next screen gives you the chance to search your e-mail address book to see if any of your contacts are already on Facebook; then, if you wish, you can invite some or all of them to become your Facebook friends.

Finding friends is covered in more detail shortly, so for the time being click **Skip this step** as shown on the bottom right above. The next step allows you, if you wish, to enter basic profile information, i.e. **Secondary School**, **University** and **Employer**. You can add to your profile or edit it at any time in the future. Click **Skip** to move on or, if you have entered any of your profile information, click **Save & continue**.

The final step in signing up to Facebook allows you to add a **Profile picture**, as shown below.

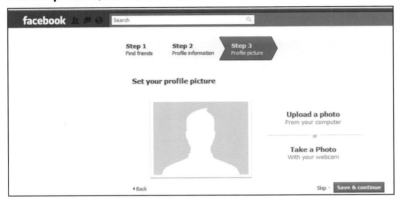

This requires you to have a suitable photo stored on your hard disc or on some other medium such as CD or memory stick (also known as a flash drive or "dongle"). Or you can upload a photo directly to Facebook if you have a webcam attached to your computer. If you don't have a suitable photo to hand you can click **Skip** to move on. (A profile photo can easily be added later). Alternatively click **Save & continue** if you have added a photo to your profile. This leads to the completion of the sign-up process discussed on the next page.

Working With Photographs

Displaying photographs for others to see is an important aspect of Facebook. If you have photos on glossy paper they will need to be scanned and then saved on your hard disc or other storage medium. You can buy an inexpensive multi-function (MFP) inkjet or laser printer which has a built-in scanner.

Many new laptop computers are now supplied with a built-in webcam. Alternatively a webcam can now be bought for a few pounds and simply plugged into one of the small rectangular USB ports on the computer.

Completing the Sign-Up Process

You should now find in your e-mail inbox a confirmation message from the Facebook team. This includes a link which you click to complete the sign-up process. You will then have a Facebook presence on the Web, as shown below open at the **Welcome** screen. This allows you to start searching for friends, as discussed on the next page. You also have the chance to upload a **Profile picture** or search for former schoolmates or colleagues, with a view to inviting them to become friends.

The previous pages have given an overview of the procedure for becoming a member of Facebook. The next few pages give more details about finding people who you may wish to invite to become Facebook friends. The next chapter describes how to build your Facebook **Profile** containing your personal information.

Finding Friends

If you click the **Find friends** button shown on the previous page you are then required to enter the password for your e-mail account with a service such as Outlook, AOL, etc. It's a good idea to change your e-mail password at regular intervals if you are worried about anyone reading your confidential information.

When you click **Sign in** shown above, Facebook searches the list of contacts in your e-mail address book and produces a list of those who are members of Facebook. You then select with a tick those contacts that you want to be your friends, as shown below.

Click the **Add** button and you can then send out invitations to contacts who you want to be your friends.

Searching Other E-mail Accounts

If you have more than one e-mail account you can search all of your address books for potential friends. Select **Find friends** and a list of popular e-mail services is displayed. In the example below, **btinternet.com** has been selected.

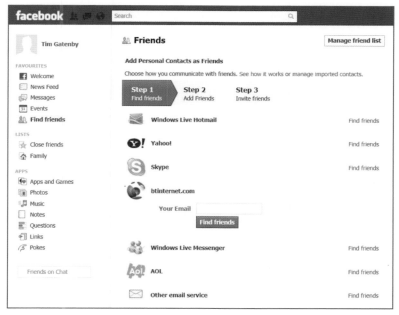

Now enter your e-mail address for that service and click **Find friends** before signing into the service, in this case **btinternet.com**, with your user name and password. The list of your contacts with this e-mail service who are members of Facebook will be displayed, similar to the list at the bottom of page 10. You can then send invitations to any of these contacts who you wish to be your Facebook friends, as previously described.

Logging In to Facebook

You are now a member of Facebook and can log in whenever you want to using your e-mail address and password on the Facebook Welcome page as described on pages 5 and 6. As discussed earlier, this page can be opened by typing the address **www.facebook.com** into the Address Bar of your Web browser.

Creating a Desktop Icon for Facebook

With the Welcome page open, right-click anywhere over the page. From the menu which pops up select **Create Shortcut**. Then click **Yes** when you are asked if you want to place a shortcut to the Web site on your Windows Desktop. The icon is then placed on your Windows Desktop. In future, to open the Facebook Welcome page quickly whenever you like, simply double-click the Desktop icon as shown on the right.

Creating Your Own Web Address for Facebook

With your own unique Facebook Web address or URL (Uniform Resource Locator) your friends, etc., can connect more easily to your pages on Facebook. They simply enter your URL into the Address Bar of their Web browser, as shown in the example for Samuel Johnson at the bottom of the page.

To create your own URL, enter **http://www.facebook.com/ username** into the Address Bar of your Web browser. For security purposes you must enter your mobile phone number. Then a confirmation code will be sent by SMS text message to the phone. Enter the confirmation code and click **Confirm**.

Then either accept the username suggested by Facebook or enter one of your own and click **Check Availability**. If your chosen name has already been used you will need to modify it, e.g. by adding a digit (0-9). Click **Confirm** to create your unique URL similar to the one shown in the example below.

http://www.facebook.com/samueljohnson

2

Building Your Profile

Introduction

This chapter looks at the task of creating your *profile*. The profile allows you to enter information about yourself and is presented in the form of a *timeline* showing the major events in your life in chronological order. If you enter lots of your personal (and possibly sensitive) information without setting the *privacy controls*, it may be viewable by everyone who uses Facebook. You can edit your profile later at any time, so if in doubt, it's a good idea not to enter confidential information until you are familiar with the privacy controls, discussed in detail starting on page 23.

The Profile Forms

Sign up to Facebook as discussed in Chapter 1, then click your name on the top right of the page and select **Edit Profile** as shown on the right.

On the left of the **Edit Profile** screen a list of the various profile forms appears, as shown here on the right. These are discussed in the next few pages. Profile pictures and photographs are also discussed again later.

> There is a link to privacy settings shown in blue on the bottom right and these are discussed in Chapter 3.

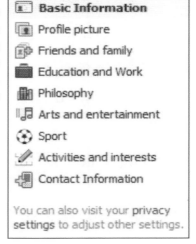

Basic Information

The first of the forms, **Basic Information**, is shown below. At this stage you can leave some of the boxes blank if you wish.

The small icons shown above and on the right are the *inline audience selectors*, used to control who sees what information, as discussed shortly. The drop-down menu below the **Birthday** boxes allows you to hide some or all of your date of birth.

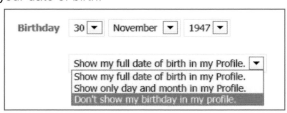

After entering your **Basic Information** click the **Save Changes** button at the bottom of the form shown above.

Adding a Profile Picture

Facebook makes it easy to add a photograph of yourself to your profile. If friends do a search after entering your name in the **Search** bar shown below, they may find a long list of people with the same name as you. The Profile photograph will enable them to identify your particular Facebook page. You can add a Profile picture during the building of your profile from the **Welcome** screen as shown below. Alternatively leave it blank and add one later after selecting **Home** (as shown on page 13) and **Welcome**.

Uploading a Photo From Your Computer

As shown above on the right, there are two ways to insert a photograph into your profile. *Uploading* means transferring a photo from your computer to a Facebook *Web server,* a powerful computer on the Internet. To use **Upload a photo** you must already have the photo stored on your hard disc or on some other storage medium, such as a *flash drive* (also known as a *memory stick*) or a CD or DVD. You can also upload photographs to Facebook from a digital camera connected to your computer. This can be done using a cable between the camera and one of the small rectangular *USB ports* (connecting sockets) on the computer. Alternatively take the *memory card* out of the camera and place it in a *card reader*. Many new computers, especially laptops, and also some printers, now have a built-in memory card reader.

If you need to use an existing photograph printed on photo paper, this will need to be *scanned* and saved on your hard disc or other medium.

Click **Upload a photo** as shown on the previous page and the following window appears, allowing you to **Browse...**, i.e. search, your hard disc and other storage devices, for the required photo.

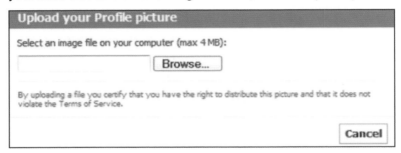

In this particular example, the required photo, **Jill and the boys** had been scanned and was stored in a folder called **Family photos** on the hard disc drive **(C:)**, as shown below.

Click the required file name in the window as shown above and then click the **Open** button at the bottom of the window. You then have to wait a short time while the picture is uploaded to your Facebook Web page on the Internet.

After a few seconds, the photograph appears as Jill's Profile picture on her Facebook **Welcome** page as shown below.

Taking a Photo With a Webcam

If you want to use an up-to-date photograph for your Profile picture, this can easily be achieved using a *webcam*. This is a small camera which can take photos and send them straight to a Web site on the Internet. Many new laptop computers have a webcam built into the top of the screen; for a desktop computer you can buy a separate webcam for a few pounds. This has a cable which plugs into one of the USB ports on the computer. Installing a separate webcam is simply a case of "plug and play" — after a few seconds the camera is ready to use.

When you click **Take a Photo** as shown on the screenshot above, the word **Loading** appears followed by the small **Take a Profile picture** window shown on the right. Click the blue camera icon at the bottom of the window and set up the photo you want. Then click the **Save picture** button at the bottom of the window. The picture then appears on your Facebook pages as shown on the next page.

The Thumbnail Version of Your Profile Photo

A thumbnail is a miniature version of a photograph. For example, when you use the Facebook **Search** bar to find a person from their name, there may be a long list of people found with the same name. If they have uploaded a Profile photo the thumbnail will appear next to their name, enabling the correct person to be identified. Click your name on the right of the Facebook blue bar, select **Edit Profile** and then click **Profile picture** on the left-hand side of the screen. Click **Edit thumbnail** and the window opens as shown below, allowing you to adjust the position of your photo by dragging with the left-hand mouse button held down.

Then click the **Save** button shown above. Your thumbnail image is displayed around the various Facebook pages, helping other people to identify you.

Friends and Family

Select **Friends and family** from the left-hand side of the screen as shown below, displayed after clicking **Edit Profile** as discussed earlier. In this form you can state whether you are married, single, in a relationship, etc., by selecting from the drop-down menu next to **Relationship Status**. You can also add family members and include their relationship (son, daughter, mother, father, etc.,) by selecting from the drop-down menu on the bar initially showing **Select Relation**.

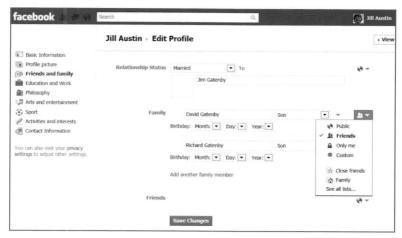

If you want to include further relatives click **Add another family member**, shown above. This produces further blank boxes under **Family** as shown above with **David** and **Richard**.

The privacy of each item of information in the **Friends and family** form shown above can be controlled using the menu obtained by clicking the *audience selector* icon shown above and on the right. Privacy is discussed in more detail in the next chapter.

Finally click the **Save Changes** button.

Education and Work

This form allows you to enter your employment details, the schools you attended and any universities. Initially there are only single bars for you to enter your employer, school or university. After you enter an employer the form expands as shown below so that you can add further details such as your position, location and how long you have worked with the company, etc.

You can add further employers, schools and universities using the blue buttons such as **Add job**, **Add school**, etc. This information can be used to renew friendships with former friends and colleagues, but you can leave boxes blank if you prefer.

Your Facebook pages can be found by anyone entering your name into the Facebook Search bar but how much they can actually see is determined by your privacy settings. By default, some Profile items are set to be viewable by everyone (the **Public** setting) unless you change them, e.g. to **Friends**, using the audience selector menu shown above and on page 19.

Philosophy

Continuing with the list of profile forms, the **Philosophy** form can be opened from the menu on the left of the screen and shown here on the right. On this form you can, if you wish, enter your religion including a description. There are similar spaces for your political views, people who inspire you and your favourite quotations. As mentioned previously, you can, if you wish, leave sections blank. (You can edit your profile at a later stage whenever you want.).

▣ Basic Information
▣ Profile picture
▣ Friends and family
▣ Education and Work
▦ **Philosophy**
♫ Arts and entertainment
☺ Sport
✎ Activities and interests
▤ Contact Information
You can also visit your **privacy settings** to adjust other settings.

Arts and Entertainment

Here you can enter your favourite music, films, books, games and television programmes, etc.

Sport

If you're interested in sport you can enter any games that you play, teams that you support and your favourite athletes.

Activities and Interests

This section can include any of the (legal) hobbies and things you like doing, such as sky diving, gardening, cooking, photography, etc.

WARNING!

The personal information above helps Facebook to put you in touch with like-minded people. However, depending on your privacy settings, (discussed in Chapter 3), people who you do not know may also be able to see your personal interests and opinions.

Contact Information

This page keeps your friends up-to-date with your latest e-mail address, web site, phone numbers and home address.

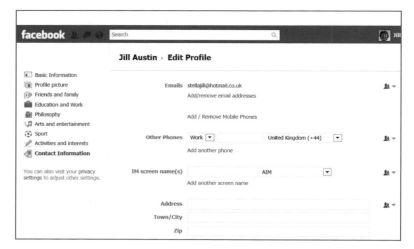

Keeping Your Own E-mail Address – Not facebook.com

During 2012, Facebook changed the e-mail addresses which users had entered in their contact details. This meant that instead of something like **johnsmith@live.co.uk**, you would now see **johnsmith@facebook.com**. This will cause any e-mails arising from your use of Facebook to be delivered to your **facebook.com** inbox, not your normal e-mail inbox.

If you prefer people to see and use your chosen e-mail service, rather than **facebook.com** e-mail, click **About** on the left of your **Profile page** and **Edit** in **Contact info**. Then use the small menu on the right of each e-mail address to select whether the address will be **Shown** or **Hidden** on your Facebook Timeline.

3

Protecting Your Privacy

Introduction

The previous chapter showed how you could start building your *Profile*, giving your basic personal information and also details of your education, career, interests and beliefs. You can enter as much or as little information as you like and you can edit your profile by adding, removing or amending information at any time in the future. As discussed later in this book, Facebook presents your biographical and contact Profile information in the form of a *Timeline*, from your birth to the present day. The Timeline lists the major events in your life in chronological order and can be illustrated with photos and video clips.

The Profile or Timeline contains a great deal of your personal and perhaps sensitive information. A major function of Facebook is to put you in touch with people with whom you may wish to share information as Facebook *friends*. In this context, friends may include close personal friends and family who you know and trust; it may also include people you don't know and have never met. These people are simply contacts who have agreed to share information and communicate through the exchange of *updates* and *messages* giving them your latest news.

Your Facebook friends may include a wide variety of people, with whom you may have quite different relationships. You may not wish them all to see every piece of profile information or news. For example, you may have a Facebook friend who is a work colleague with whom you share information for business or professional reasons. You may not want to share with them details of your private or family life. Similarly someone may not want a former spouse or partner to know details about their new relationships.

Or a young person might not want their parents to see the information that they would share with their young friends (and vice-versa).

However, without suitable safeguards, people who are not your friends may be able to find your Facebook pages and read your personal information without your permission. Anyone who has signed up and joined Facebook can type in a name (such as yours) into the blue Search bar at the top of the screen, as shown below.

Clicking the magnifying glass icon on the right above produces a list of people with the name you entered, as shown below.

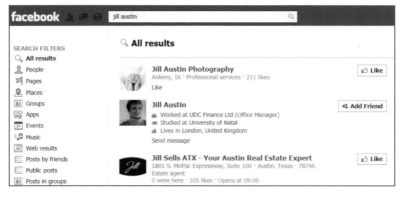

A person who is not your friend can select your name from the list as shown above and see your personal information. They will also see a list of your friends names and clicking on these may reveal your friends' information.

As there are currently over one billion users on Facebook, you may not want some of them to be able to find your Web pages. Just as there are some people you wouldn't want to know your contact details or the dates when you are going on holiday (and leaving your house empty).

Privacy Settings

There are various settings that you can use to prevent people who are not your friends from seeing your personal information. However, many of these are initially set to give *Public* access, i.e. visible to anyone and everyone using Facebook. Unless you alter these privacy settings, as described below, anyone can see all of your information.

Inline Audience Selectors

These allow you to control who sees what items of information in your profile (timeline) and any status updates you post on Facebook. The audience selector is an icon which appears next to many of the boxes where you enter your profile information. It also appears next to the boxes where you enter status updates. When you click the icon, a drop-down menu appears as shown below on the right. This lists the various privacy settings such as **Public**, **Friends**, **Only me**, **Custom** and **Close Friends**.

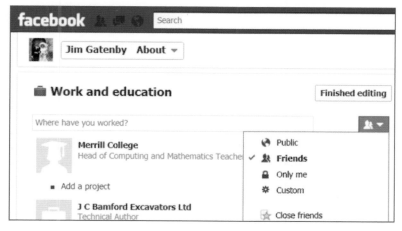

After setting the privacy, the selected icon appears next to the information, as shown for **Friends** above and on the right.

When you pass the cursor over the audience selector icon, the privacy setting appears against a black background, as shown by **Friends** on the right.

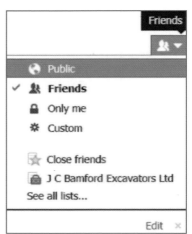

As shown at the bottom right, you can **Edit** or amend a piece of information in your Profile. Clicking the small cross on the bottom right removes the information from your Profile. The Privacy settings are described in more detail below:

Public

This is the maximum audience for your information, which will be visible to anyone who finds your pages on Facebook. Many Profile information boxes are initially set with the **Public** privacy icon by default. You should review these carefully and, if necessary, change the privacy setting using the above menu.

If an item of information does not have an adjacent audience selector icon, assume it is **Public**. For example, certain parts of your Profile are always **Public**. These include your name, gender, Profile picture, any school or work networks you belong to and your username. These are always set at **Public** to enable people to find and identify you and possibly send you a friend request. If you're not happy with any of this information being **Public**, don't include it in your Profile in the first place. If you decide to remove any existing **Public** information in your Profile click the small cross shown in the top screenshot, on the right of the word **Edit**.

Friends

Information tagged with the **Friends** setting will be visible to all the people with whom you have agreed to share your information, by accepting their request for you to be **Friends**.

Only Me

It may be convenient to store some information on Facebook which is only visible to yourself.

Custom

Clicking this privacy setting opens a window offering a range of options, as shown below. You can tailor access to a piece of information so that it is only visible to specific people or lists of people. Alternatively the **Custom** icon can be used to hide the information from certain people or lists of people, as shown below.

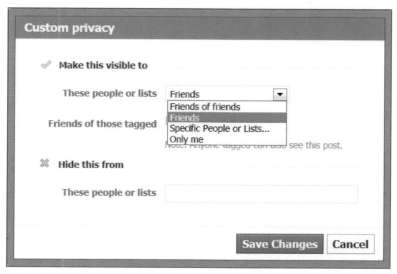

After setting the privacy of an item of information using **Custom privacy**, click the **Save Changes** button to make it permanent.

Who Can See What?

The **View As** feature in Facebook allows you to check how much of your Profile information is visible to different categories of user. This depends on the privacy settings you have made using the audience selectors discussed on the previous pages. Click your name on the top right-hand side of the blue Facebook bar .

This opens your Profile (Timeline) as shown below. Since you are logged in as yourself on this computer, the screen displays all of your Profile.

To see how other people can view your Profile, click the downward pointing arrow to the right of **Activity log**, shown above and then select **View As** from the small drop-down menu
shown on the right. Part of your Profile (Timeline) is displayed, as shown at the top of the next page, under the heading **This is how your Timeline looks to the public**. In this example; because I have used the audience selectors to set my education and work details as **Friends** only, the public (i.e. people who are not friends) can only see my name, Profile picture and gender. As stated earlier, your name, Profile picture and gender are always visible to everyone on Facebook.

Towards the top left of the above screen extract, there is a box allowing you to **Enter a friend's name**.

Enter one of your Facebook friend's names in the box and you will see how much of your profile information is visible to them. As shown below under **This is how your timeline looks to Jill Gatenby**, your friends may see all of your profile information, depending on your privacy settings made with the audience selectors. These privacy settings can be changed at any time.

Further Privacy Settings

You can make further changes
to the way other people can
view and interact with your
Facebook pages after clicking
the **Privacy Settings** option
shown on the right. This menu

is displayed after clicking the small downward arrow on the right
of **Home** in the top right-hand corner of the Facebook screen.

Shown at the top of the **Privacy settings** window below is the
inline audience selector, as discussed previously. This is used
when creating or editing your profile or when posting status
updates to your wall. The three icons shown below allow you to
apply a default privacy setting in situations where there is no
audience selector, such as posts to your Facebook Profile
(Timeline) from a Blackberry smartphone.

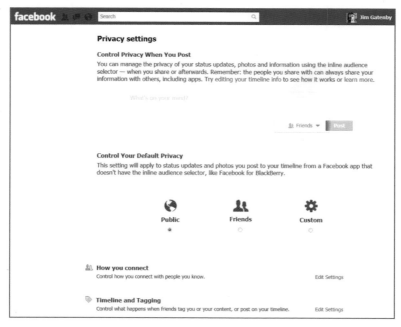

If you select **Edit Settings** to the right of **How you connect** at the bottom of the previous page, the following window appears.

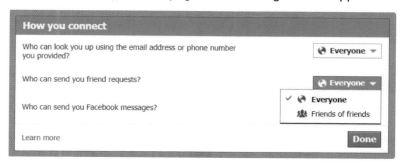

Using the drop-down menus shown in the example above, you can specify how other people are allowed to interact with your Facebook site. This includes finding you from your e-mail address and phone number, sending you friend requests and Facebook messages (discussed shortly).

The Facebook Help Centre

Comprehensive help facilities are available after clicking **Help** from the menu shown at the top right of the previous page and then selecting **Visit the Help Center**. Apart from entering questions for help, all major Facebook features are explained and there is a glossary of Facebook terms.

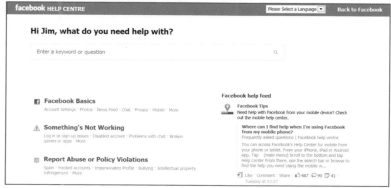

Summary: Profile (Timeline) and Privacy

- Your Facebook profile allows you to enter personal information such as a photograph, your gender, date of birth, details of your family, education, employment, hobbies, interests and contact details.

- You can start building your profile immediately after signing up for Facebook but it can be edited at any time in the future using **Update info** and **Edit**.

- Your profile picture can be added to Facebook by uploading a photo stored on your hard disc drive, etc., or posted directly from a webcam attached to your computer.

- A thumbnail or miniature version of your photograph can be displayed on various pages on the Facebook site. This helps friends to know they are communicating with you and not someone else with the same name as you.

- The information on your profile can be used to put you in touch with people with similar interests and background who you may wish to invite to be your Facebook friends.

- Privacy settings should be used to control who can see your information; otherwise people you do not know may find you on Facebook and view confidential information.

- *Inline audience selectors* are privacy settings which control who can share which parts of your information such as your age, contact details, religious beliefs, etc. Various levels of privacy can be set such as **Public** (accessible to everyone logged on to Facebook), **Friends**, **Custom** (specific people) and **Only me**.

- Some information such as name, gender, education and your profile photograph is always **Public**, i.e. shareable by everyone, so that it can be used to assist in the finding of people you may wish to invite to become friends.

4

Finding Friends

Facebook Friends

The term *friends* on Facebook covers all the people you communicate with; this includes close personal friends as well as members of your family and colleagues from work and perhaps your student days. You can invite people to be your friend and they can accept or reject the invitation. Similarly you will be invited by other people to be their friend.

There are various methods used by Facebook to help you find people who you might want as friends, such as:

- Facebook scans your e-mail contacts to find people who are already on Facebook and suggests them as friends.

- Your e-mail contacts who are not already members of Facebook may be sent an invitation to join.

- From your profile information, Facebook suggests people having something in common with you, such as your home district, school, college or employer. You can also initiate a search to find people with similar profile information and interests.

- If you think that someone may already be a member of Facebook, you can enter their name into the Search bar in Facebook. If their name is not too common you should be able to find their page quickly from the list of search results, especially if they have included a profile picture.

- You are advised that Facebook users should not invite complete strangers to be friends or accept an invitation to be the friend of someone they don't know.

Finding Friends From E-mail Contacts

Your e-mail address is used in Facebook as your log-in name; then Facebook can scan your e-mail address book or contacts list and find any of your contacts who are members of Facebook. This enables Facebook to suggest people who may wish to be your friends. Any of your contacts who are not members may be sent an invitation to join Facebook. You can initiate a search of your e-mail contacts after clicking **Find friends** from the blue menu bar across the top right of the Facebook screen.

Make sure your e-mail address appears in the slot labelled **Your Email** in the highlighted e-mail service such as **Windows Live Hotmail** in the example above. Then click the **Find friends** button shown above.

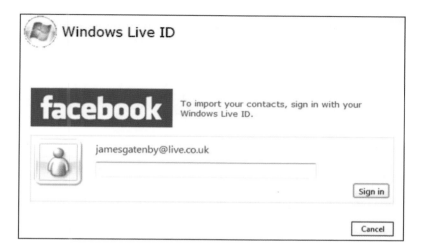

Next enter your e-mail address and password for the e-mail service. After you click **Find friends**, the following window appears:

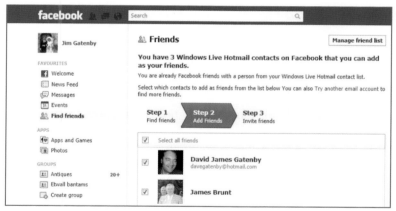

After a few seconds anyone in the contacts list for that e-mail service who is a member of Facebook will be displayed. You can, if you wish, click the small box next to the thumbnail picture and select **Add Friends** if you want to send them an invitation.

Accepting or Declining a Friend Request

When a user logs in to Facebook, they will see any requests to be their friend; they can then click either **Confirm** or **Not now**, to accept or decline the offer of friendship, as shown below.

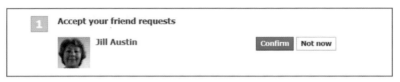

If a user clicks the **Not now** button shown above, they are asked if they know the person requesting their friendship. If they don't know them, they should click **No**. Facebook will then stop that person from sending them any more requests.

Using an Unlisted E-mail Service

If you use an e-mail service other than those listed on page 34, click **Other email service** near the bottom of the list. Then enter your e-mail address and password for that service and click **Find friends**. Any of your contacts on that e-mail service who are members of Facebook will be invited to be your friend. These contacts can then either accept or reject your friend request.

Using an E-mail Contact File

At the bottom of the list on page 34 there is a link entitled **Other tools**. Click this link and a list of searches is displayed, based on your Profile information, as discussed in Chapter 2.

 Other tools

Upload contact file

Find classmates from Bemrose School »

Find university friends, past or present »

Find former colleagues from Merrill College »

Upload contact file above means *importing* to Facebook a file of your e-mail contacts from an e-mail service which is not recognised by Facebook.

Creating a Contact File

First you must create the file by *exporting* the list of contacts from your e-mail program. The file of e-mail contacts takes the form of a *CSV* (*Comma Separated Variables*) text file. The precise method for creating a CSV contacts file varies for different e-mail programs but the general method is as follows:

- Open the e-mail program.
- From the **File** menu select **Export**.
- Click **Accounts**.
- Click the name of the required e-mail account.
- Click the **Export** button.
- Select a folder on the hard disc drive to save the file.
- Give the file a name. If necessary select *.csv* as the file type.
- Click the **Save** button to place a copy of the file on your hard disc drive.

Uploading an E-mail Contact File

As stated earlier, the contacts file only needs to be created if Facebook can't search your e-mail address book to find your contacts who are also members of Facebook. This may occur if your e-mail service uses an *e-mail client program* based on your hard disc rather than a Web-based system such as Hotmail.

Having created a CSV file of your e-mail contacts on your hard disc as previously described, it now has to be imported or uploaded to the Facebook web site. Click **Find friends** from the blue bar across the top of the Facebook screen. Then under **Other tools**, select **Upload contact file**. Next click the **Browse** button to look for and select the contact file on your hard disc.

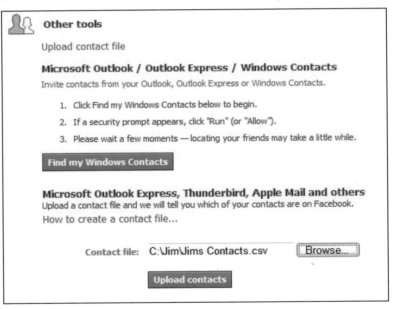

When you select **Upload contacts** shown above, Facebook lists those of your e-mail contacts who are members of Facebook and gives you the options to **Send invitations** or **Skip**.

Searching Using Profile Information

When you click **Other tools** as shown on the **Friends** window below, apart from the **Upload contact file** just discussed, Facebook displays a number of searches to find people you may have known in the past and who are members of Facebook.

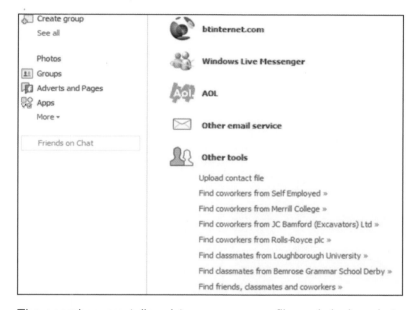

The searches are tailored to your own profile and designed to find Facebook members from your old school, college or employment, etc., as shown in the examples above, all starting with the word **Find**.

Clicking any of the **Find** options shown above produces a list of people whose backgrounds have something in common with yours. Any of the people listed whose thumbnails you recognise can, if you wish, be invited to be friends by clicking **Add Friend**. Obviously a good profile picture enables you to be sure you know the person listed.

If you click **Find friends, classmates and co-workers** shown on the previous page, a list of people is displayed under the heading **Find friends from different parts of your life**. Depending on the amount of information you have entered in your profile, this may be an enormous list. This list is the sum total of all the people on Facebook who are connected to you in some way, based on all of your profile information, your friends and friends of friends.

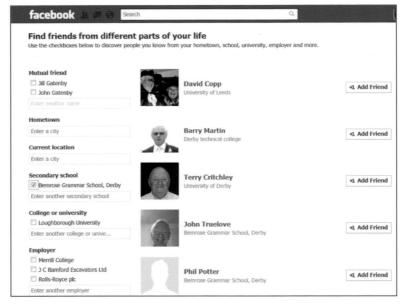

Tick boxes on the left of the screen allow you to filter out people from different parts of your life. Ticking more than one box will narrow down the search; for example, to find people who went to school with you and who

now live in the same town, etc. Click **Add Friend** to send them an invitation.

Searching for a Name

The Search Bar at the top of the Facebook Home Page allows you to enter the name of a person and search for them amongst all the members of Facebook.

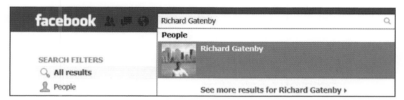

Click the link **See more results for ...** shown above to display all of the people with that name or click the small magnifying glass. Unless the name is very unusual, you will find a long list of people with the required name. If they have included a recent profile picture you should be able to identify their record and click **Add Friend** to send them an invitation.

If you're not able to recognise the person you want on the list, try clicking the names in blue. One of the records may display some information which confirms them as the person you're seeking.

You can also type the name of a personality, community, business or television programme. For example, entering **Rolls-Royce** into the search bar produces several results giving information about the various Rolls-Royce companies. Popular television programmes may have Facebook pages to which people have posted their opinions. These can include video clips enabling you to watch repeats of programmes on your computer.

Sending and Receiving Friend Requests

If your name appears on someone's Facebook page, they can click the **Add Friend** button, as shown on the previous page, to send you a friend request.

Friend requests appear on your **Welcome** page, as shown below. This can be displayed after clicking **Home** from the blue bar at the top of the Facebook screen.

Then click **Welcome** from the left-hand panel.

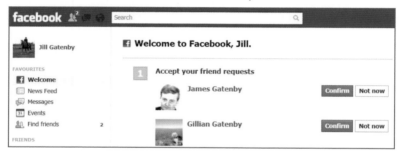

To accept a person as a Facebook friend, click the **Confirm** button, shown above. Otherwise click **Not now**. As discussed on page 31, the Facebook privacy settings allow you some control over who can send you friend requests. Click the downward pointing arrow next to **Home**, select **Privacy Settings** and then **Edit Settings** on the right of **How you connect**. Then select **Everyone** or **Friends of friends**. Friend requests are also displayed when you click the small people icon next to the word **facebook** on the left of the Facebook blue bar.

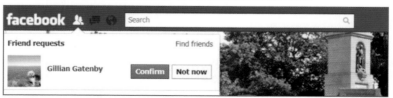

Removing a Facebook Friend

If you no longer want to exchange news and information with a friend on Facebook, you can remove or "unfriend" them. This can be done from your Profile (Timeline), discussed in more detail shortly, or from your Home page. Both of these show photographs of your friends. To open your Profile, click your name on the blue Facebook bar, as shown near the top of the previous page. Alternatively click **Home** and **FRIENDS**.

Allow the cursor to hover over the profile photo of the friend you wish to remove. The window shown on the upper right appears. Now allow the cursor to hover over the **Friends** button, as shown on the top window. The drop-down window shown on the lower right appears from which you click **Unfriend**.

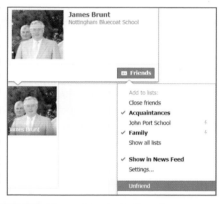

Select the **Remove from Friends** button to complete the process or select **Cancel** if you change your mind.

Organising Friends into Lists

To make it simpler to manage your friends you can organise them into various lists, such as *Close Friends*, *Acquaintances*, and *Restricted*. These lists are provided by default by Facebook. People in these lists will see differing amounts of your posts on Facebook. Close Friends are your best friends and will appear regularly in your News Feeds (discussed shortly) and see all of your posts. Acquaintances are people you don't wish to be in constant contact with and they can be excluded from your posts. People on your Restricted list can only see your Public posts and information, as discussed in Chapter 3.

Smart lists are lists which are created automatically by Facebook, based on profile information such as your town, education and employment details. When you acquire friends whose profile information matches a list, their names are added to the smart list. You can also create new lists of your own, as discussed shortly.

Log on to Facebook and click **Find friends** from the right-hand side of the blue bar at the top of the screen, as shown below.

Click **Manage friend list** shown above to display a list of all friends. Click a friend's name to open their Profile (Timeline) and click the **Friends** button. This displays a drop-down menu of various lists of friends, such as **Acquaintances**, **Family** and lists related to education and employment, as shown on the next page.

To add the selected friend to a list, click the name of the list, such as **Family** or **Restricted** for example.

If you click **Restricted**, as shown on the right, the person concerned can only view profile information to which you have assigned the **Public** setting, as described in the previous chapter.

As shown on the right, you can click **+New List** to create a new list of your own, or display the names of further lists of Facebook friends by clicking

Show all lists. There is also an option to click **Unfriend** to remove the selected person as a Facebook friend.

Removing a Friend from a List (but not from Facebook)

Click **Home** from the top right of the screen, then select **FRIENDS** and **MORE** and click the name of list in the centre panel. Then select **Manage List** and **Edit List** and click the friend's name to remove them from the list.

Creating a New List

To display the names of your lists in the left-hand panel, click **Home** from the right-hand side of the top blue bar. Then from the left-hand panel click **FRIENDS**, as shown below. Then click the **+Create List** button as shown below and enter a **List name** of your own choosing. Next enter the names of the people who are to be on the list and click the **Create** button. Facebook suggests on a drop-down menu the names of people who you may wish to click to add them to the new list, as shown below.

Then click the **Create** button to save the list. The name of newly created list will now appear in the left-hand panel of your **Home** screen, as shown on the right in the case of the new list called **Milton**. With the list selected in the left-hand panel you can quickly view the members pages, or edit or remove the list using **Manage list**.

Using Lists to Control Your Privacy

Chapter 3 showed how you can use the *audience selector* to control who can see your profile information and the news and status updates you post on your Facebook pages. Your Friends Lists are included on the drop-down menu under the audience selector icon. In the example below, the newly created list **Milton** can be selected, allowing people who are on the list (but not on the Restricted list) to view the **Work and education** information.

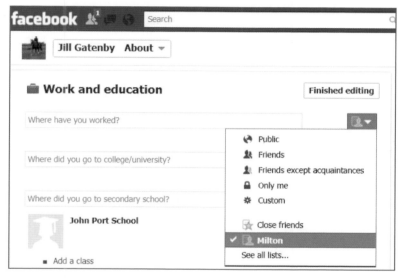

As discussed shortly, a major feature of Facebook is the ability to post *status updates* giving your latest news and photos, etc. This can be done from your Profile (Timeline), obtained by clicking your name on the blue Facebook bar. If you click the audience selector icon, the drop-down menu appears, similar to the one above. Then click **See all lists** and click (and tick) a list of friends with whom you wish to share the update.

Alternatively, on your **Home** page, select the list from the left-hand panel, as shown on page 46. Then proceed to write your update, adding any photos or videos.

As shown below, the list (**Milton**) which has been selected in the left-hand panel, is used to control the viewing audience, as shown by the audience selector on the left of the **Post** button.

Alternatively, when sending a status update, instead of selecting the list in the left-hand panel, select it from the drop-down menu obtained by clicking the audience selector icon.

Blocking Users

You can use the **Block** feature to prevent people from seeing your profile. Click the small arrow on the right of **Home** on the right of the Facebook blue bar. From the drop-down menu select **Privacy Settings** and from the bottom of the privacy settings screen, select **Manage blocking** on the right-hand side.

As shown below, you can enter the names of people who you no longer want as friends and stop them sending you invitations to future events or interacting with you in applications (programs).

5

Using Facebook

Introduction

Earlier chapters looked at the setting up of a new Facebook account and the entry of information about yourself in your Profile (Timeline). The previous chapter showed how to search your e-mail contacts lists for people who are members of Facebook and how they may accept or reject your request to become a Facebook friend. This chapter shows how you can start to use Facebook to communicate with friends.

Signing In

Open the Facebook sign-in page by entering the address **www.facebook.com** into the address bar of your Web browser or by double-clicking an icon on the Windows Desktop as discussed on pages 6 and 12. Then enter your e-mail address and password as shown below and click the **Log in** button.

If you are the only person who uses this particular computer, you may wish to click the box next to **Keep me logged in** to place a tick in it. However, if you do tick the box, other people with access to the computer who are not your friends may be able to read information which you'd rather not share with them.

After you click the **Log in** button, Facebook opens with your **Home** page displaying your **News Feed**, as shown on the next page. Your News Feed displays recent Facebook activity and exchanges of information between you and your friends. These exchanges are known as *status updates* or *posts*.

Navigating Around Facebook

The blue bar shown below is always present across the top of the Facebook screen. On the left of the bar, the word **facebook** (in white) can be clicked to return to your **Home** page (including your **News Feed**) at any time.

To the right of the word **facebook** above there are three icons, normally  very faint but shown in white on the right for the sake of clarity. These icons can be clicked to find out if there are any **Friend requests**, new **Messages** or **Notifications**. These topics are discussed elsewhere in this book. As discussed shortly, Messages are different from News Feeds. Messages are shared between you and one or more named contacts, in a similar way to an e-mail. News Feeds can be viewed by friends, friends of friends or everyone, depending on your privacy settings, as discussed in Chapter 3.

Across the top right of the screen, the blue Facebook bar has three major features, as shown below.

Clicking your name on the blue bar shown above opens your Profile (Timeline) as discussed in detail shortly. The **Find friends** feature was discussed in Chapter 4.

If you click **Home** shown above, your Home page opens with your **News Feed** feature selected as shown at the top of the next page. This shows any recent posts or updates from your friends or posted by yourself.

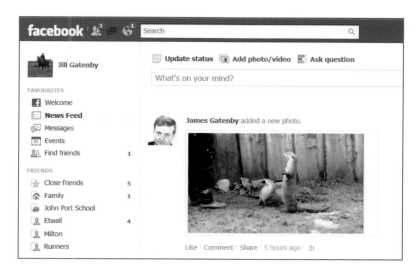

On the right of the blue Facebook bar there is a small downward pointing arrow, to the right of the word **Home** as shown below. Click the arrow to open the drop-down menu also shown below.

The **Advertise** option shown on the right provides information for people wanting to use Facebook to promote themselves or their business. **Account Settings** allows you to edit details such as your username, e-mail address and

password and any Facebook networks you belong to. **Privacy Settings** were discussed in detail in Chapter 3. **Log out** takes you back to the **Log in** screen shown on page 49.

The **Help** option shown above opens many pages explaining all aspects of Facebook, including the **Help Centre** and a **Glossary of Terms**. Several videos are provided covering important new features, such as the Profile (Timeline), introduced in 2011 – 2012 and discussed on the next page.

Your Profile (Timeline)

Chapter 2 described the building of your Profile by entering your personal information such as details of your education, employment and interests. The Profile has always been at the centre of Facebook as it is used to bring together like-minded people sharing common interests and experiences. Then by agreeing to become Facebook friends they can share news and information. Facebook friends can also include close personal friends and family who want to keep in touch while living apart in far flung corners of the world.

At the time of writing in 2012, the Profile has undergone a major redesign which is being made available progressively to users in a rolling program. Although the user still creates their profile by filling in forms on the screen, Facebook presents all of this information in the form of a *Timeline*, giving the events in your life in chronological order from your birth upwards.

You can display your Profile (Timeline) by clicking your name on the top right of the blue Facebook bar, or wherever it appears on the screen. Across the top of the Profile (Timeline) you can insert a Cover picture as shown below. Your personal information is listed down the left-hand side.

Scrolling down the Profile (Timeline), you can see the pictures you have posted and events going back in time, to your date of birth (if you've chosen to share it).

The Profile (Timeline) incorporates your wall, which displays all the updates including text, photographs and video clips you and your friends have posted

Editing Your Profile (Timeline)
Adding a Cover Picture

Across the top of the Profile is your chosen cover picture. Initially this area is blank, but you can click the **Add a Cover** button to insert a photo. The option **Choose from photos...** is used

to select a photo that you've already placed on Facebook. **Upload a photo...** enables you to browse and select a photo from your computer's hard disc drive or a flash drive, or a camera's memory card etc.

Changing Your Cover Picture

Hovering over the cover picture displays the **Change Cover** button allowing you to use a different photograph. A post appears on your Timeline to say that you have updated your

cover, together with a small copy of the new cover. This post also appears on your friends' News Feeds. Facebook requests that your cover picture is not used as an advertising banner.

Editing Your Personal Information

Your personal information is shown below and on the bottom left of the Profile (Timeline), the main picture on the previous page.

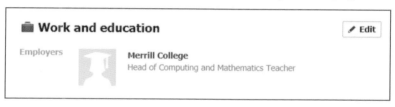

The data you have entered, such as school or place of employment, appears in blue. Click on one of the icons on the left of each line of your profile information to bring up an editing screen where you can make changes. Alternatively click the **Update info** button shown in the centre of the previous page.

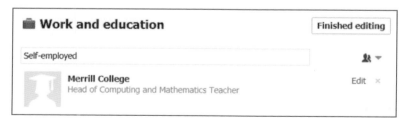

If you click the **Edit** button shown above, the profile forms appear with blank slots for you to enter the new data, such as **Self-employed** in the example below.

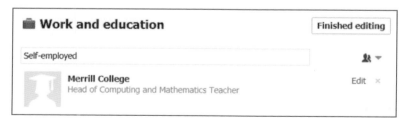

After entering your new profile data, click the **Finished editing** button shown above to save the changes you have made.

Posting an Update from Your News Feed

A status update is used to tell your Facebook friends your latest news and what you are currently doing. With **News Feed** selected, as shown below, click **Update status** near the middle of the screen. An empty box opens allowing you to enter some text in response to **What's on your mind?** As discussed on page 59, you can include a photo or video with the post.

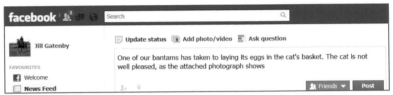

Next click the audience selector icon shown above and on the right, to the left of  the **Post** button. From the drop-down menu which appears, select who can view the status update. As discussed in the previous chapter, friends can be organised in *Lists* such as colleagues at work. To make your post viewable by people on a particular list, select **See all lists...** and then click the list. The **Custom** privacy option allows you to share the post with specific people or lists or hide it from specific people or lists. Click **Save Changes** to complete the **Custom privacy** setting.

When Jill types an update about her cat, for example, as shown on the previous page and then clicks **Post**, the update appears at the top of her News Feed, as shown below.

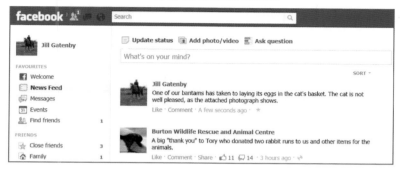

The update also appears on Jill's Profile (Timeline). Depending on the privacy settings chosen, anyone might be able to view Jill's Profile (Timeline) and will be able to see the status updates she has posted. Access to parts of your Profile (Timeline) by a person who is not your friend can be prevented using your privacy settings, as discussed in Chapter 3, page 23 onwards.

The above post was set as viewable by **Friends**. When Jill's friends, (such as James below), log on to their own Facebook Home page, they will see the latest post about Jill's cat near the top of their News Feed. James can leave a comment if desired and this will quickly be viewable on Jill's News Feed.

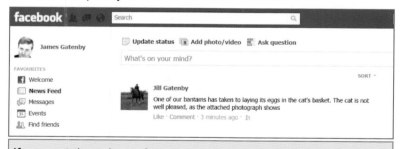

If you set the privacy for a status update at **Public**, anyone on Facebook can find your pages and view what you have posted.

Posting an Update from Your Timeline

From now on this book will refer to the Profile (Timeline) as simply the Timeline. A status update can be posted from the Timeline as shown below, as well as from the News Feed, as just discussed. If the Timeline is not on the screen, click your name on the right of the blue bar at the top of the Facebook screen.

The bar for entering a status update is located at the bottom left of the Facebook screen, as shown above. When you click inside the bar over **What's on your mind?** the status bar opens up ready for you to enter the text of your update.

Including a Photo With a Status Update

You can enhance a status update by including a photo or a video clip for example. Click **Photo** as shown at the bottom of the previous page. The following options appear.

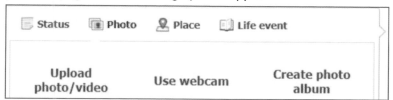

You are given the choice to upload a photo or video stored on your hard disc or from another location such as a flash drive. Or you can take a new photograph if you have a webcam. Many laptops have a built-in webcam or you can buy a separate plug-in device for a few pounds. Uploading photos and videos to Facebook using a webcam is discussed in Chapters 2 and 7.

When you select **Upload photo/video** you can then browse your hard disc, or flash drive, etc., to find the location, (folder), where the photo or video is stored. In the example below, a photo called **Bantam evicts cat** is uploaded from the folder **Jills photos** on the **C:** drive (i.e. the hard disc drive inside the computer).

Then enter the text in the bar shown above, over the words **Say something about this….** Finally click **Post** to share the update.

When you click the **Post** button, the status update consisting of the text message and photograph is posted to your Timeline and to your News Feed as shown below.

Clicking the photograph in the Timeline or News Feed enlarges it to fill most of the screen as shown below.

Posting a Web Link

If you think your friends may be interested in a particular Web site, you can send a live link as part of a status update. Click inside the status bar on your News Feed or Wall and enter the Web address, for example, **www.babanibooks.com**.

When you press Enter, the first few lines of the Web site are displayed and there is a space under the Web address for you to add some text, as shown below.

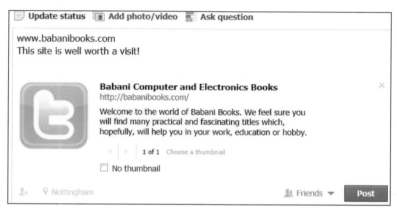

Use the audience selector to set the privacy level of the post. Then click the **Post** button shown above and the link soon appears on your friends' News Feeds, as shown below, together with your text message and the first few lines extracted from the Web site itself. A friend can then click the link, in this example www.babanibooks.com, to visit the Web site.

Some Important Features of Facebook

- Your Timeline includes details of your education, employment, likes and dislikes and contact details. The Timeline is a new version of the Facebook Profile.

- The Wall is part of your Timeline and consists of Status Updates or Posts; these are short notes on the Wall telling your friends what you are doing or thinking and also listing any changes you've made to your Timeline information.

- Updates can include photographs, videos and links to other Web sites.

- Updates appear on your News Feed and on your friends' News Feed, allowing friends to read the text, view photos and videos and open links to other Web sites.

- Photos and videos can be uploaded to Facebook from your hard disc drive or from a flash drive, or CD, etc. Alternatively new photos and videos can be prepared using a webcam attached to your computer, before being shared with your friends as posts or updates.

- Other people may write Comments on your updates or click the Like button to express agreement.

- Friends may be able to write updates on your Wall.

- You can use Audience Selectors or Privacy Settings to control who can share your personal information and the updates you post to Facebook.

- The main Privacy Settings are Public (the maximum audience, viewable by everyone), also Friends, Custom (specified people) and the most private, Only me.

- Friends can be organised into named Lists, based on education or employment, for example. The names of these lists appear on the Audience Selector menus, enabling information to be shared easily with particular sets of friends.

6

More Facebook Activities

Introduction

The last chapter described the way you can navigate around the various Facebook pages, by clicking the text links on the blue bar across the top of the Facebook screen.

Two of the main pages discussed were the Home page and the Timeline, also known as your personal Profile. Editing your personal information in the Timeline and also inserting (and changing) a Cover Picture, were also discussed.

The essential Facebook tasks of posting status updates consisting of text, photos, videos and Web links were also described. This included the use of the Audience Selectors to determine who can see the information you post on Facebook. Depending on your Privacy Settings, copies of your posts may only appear on your Friends' News Feeds. Alternatively, if the Public setting is used, posts may be available for anyone to see.

This chapter looks at some of the other features in Facebook, such as creating Messages that only specific people can read and also writing messages directly on a friend's Wall on their Timeline. The Chat facility allows you to exchange messages in real time with friends who are online, while the Poke feature is used to remind someone you still exist and are available online, perhaps for a Chat.

Finally there is a case study showing how Facebook is used by a local wildlife rescue centre, to share news and pictures and raise funds to support the work of volunteers.

Messages

This feature is different from the Status Updates described in Chapter 5. Whereas an update is posted to the Wall on your Timeline and can be viewed by and commented on by anyone with access to view your Wall, a message is sent to one or more specific people, like an e-mail. Other people will not be able to see it.

Make sure you're on your Home page by clicking **Home** on the right-hand side of the Facebook screen or by clicking the word **facebook** on the blue bar as shown below. Select **Messages** from the menu on the left of the screen, and click the **+ New message** button shown below.

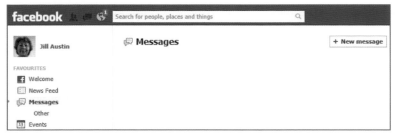

The **New message** window opens as shown below. Then enter the name(s) or e-mail address(es) of a friend or friends or the name of a Facebook List of friends as discussed in Chapter 4.

The **New message** window at the bottom of the previous page has two icons as shown on the right. The paper clip icon allows you to browse your computer for a stored file such as a photo, as described on page 59, and attach it to the message. The camera icon on the right above can be used to attach a photo or video taken with a webcam, as discussed in Chapter 7.

When Jill has finished the message, clicking **Send** will place a copy in the Message area of the recipient's Home page. Next time the recipient, in this case James, signs in to Facebook they can read the message and if necessary send a reply. An extract from James' Message area is shown below. James could send a reply by entering some text and clicking the **Reply** button.

The reply is sent to Jill's message area, where a number, displayed to the right of **Messages** shown on the right, indicates that there are new messages. On clicking **Messages** shown on the right above, the reply from James is displayed on Jill's screen. There is an option to delete selected messages on the **Actions** menu shown on the right. This menu is opened by clicking the **Actions** button, shown on the right and on the top right of the main screenshot above.

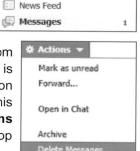

Writing on a Friend's Wall (Timeline)

You can post a message directly on a friend's Wall, an area of their Timeline. First sign in to your own Facebook account.

Then find your friend's Facebook pages by entering their name into the Search bar on the blue bar across the top of the Facebook screen. Then select your friend from the list of people found in the search. Alternatively select your friend from the list displayed after clicking **Friend**. Your friend's Timeline is displayed automatically as shown below. The extract below shows that James is logged in on this computer, since his name appears on the blue bar at the top right of the screen. However, it is Jill's Timeline which now fills the screen. At the bottom left is the Update or Status bar in which you can write something.

Now type your message on your friend's Timeline in the bar as shown below under **Post**, replacing **Write something...**.

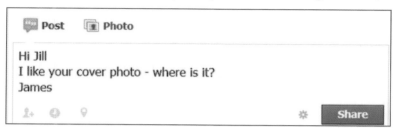

When you click **Share**, the message you've written appears as a new post at the top of your friend's Timeline as shown below.

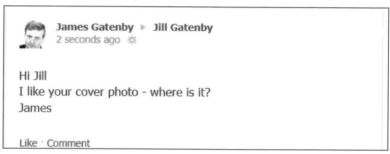

Only you and your friend's can write on the Wall area of your Timeline. Other people may be able to see some parts of your Timeline, depending on the Privacy Settings applied to your Profile information or to the posts you and your friends have made, as discussed in Chapter 3. To prevent anyone from posting on your Wall, from the **Home** menu select **Privacy Settings** and click **Edit Settings**, to the right of **Timeline and Tagging**. Then click the Audience Selector icon and select **No one** as shown below.

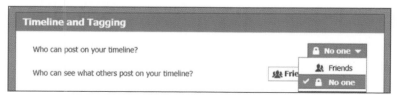

The Chat Feature

This allows you to communicate in real time, with Facebook friends who are currently online. This is done by typing text messages into a window which pops up. A small rectangle at the bottom right of the screen shows if you have any friends currently online.

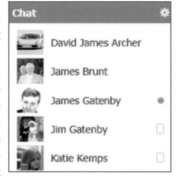

Click the **Chat** rectangle shown above to see who is online. The window shown on the right appears. The green dot indicates a friend is online, so click their name to start chatting.

A window opens for you to type in your text "conversation" at the flashing cursor in the bar at the bottom, as shown below. If you've recently sent any **Messages**, as discussed on page 64, these also appear at the top of the Chat window shown below.

When you press the **Enter** or **Return** key, the message appears in your own chat window as shown on the right. It will also appear in your friend's Chat window. As you keep entering messages they appear immediately on the screens of both parties to the conversation. A small camera icon shown above and on the right allows you

to set up video chats, enabling you to see the person you're chatting to. This requires webcams on each computer as discussed in Chapter 7.

The Poke Feature

This is a very quick and simple way of saying hello and telling someone you're online to Facebook. Log on to your Facebook Home page, then view your friend's Timeline, as discussed on page 66. Click the arrow on the right of the **Message** button to open the drop-down menu shown below. Then click **Poke**.

You then receive a notification that you have successfully poked your friend.

Your friend receives a notification of the Poke on their Home page and they are given the chance to poke you back.

You receive the return poke immediately after they send it, so you know that they must have seen your original poke.

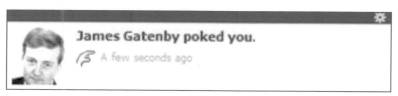

Making More Friends on Facebook

Chapter 4 showed how you can actively search for people with whom you might want to interact as friends. This includes trawling through your e-mail address books or contact lists. You can also search for people whose profile information matches your own, such as a school, employer or shared hobbies and interests.

Facebook also continually searches on your behalf, looking for people with whom you have something in common or with whom you share a mutual friend. These potential friends are listed on the Welcome section of your Home page, as shown below.

To invite someone to be a friend, click the adjacent **Add Friend** button, as shown above. Then the sending of the request is confirmed, as shown below.

The recipient can either accept or reject the request, as discussed on page 42.

A Facebook Case Study — Wildlife Rescue

We came across this Facebook site after a tawny owl flew into our car and appeared to be mortally wounded. We needed to find specialist help to save the owl's life. Fortunately a search using Google quickly led to the Facebook pages of the Burton Wildlife Rescue and Animal Centre shown below.

With their care the owl made a complete recovery and was soon released back into the wild. Clicking the above Web link opens the centre's Timeline, as shown below.

As shown on the previous page, the Timeline of the rescue centre displays posts giving news of the latest animals to be rescued and requests for help from the public.

Burton Wildlife Rescue and Animal Centre
15 May

Callout to Tamworth about a duck last night who has taken residence in a swimming pool along with 12 ducklings. We will be relocating the family to a local lake.Yesterday after 3 hours we nearly caught her so going back in an hour. Wish us luck!

The Wall on the Timeline is also used to post progress reports on the recovery of sick animals. Dogs and cats are found new homes as a result of posts on the Timeline. Members of the public are very active in placing comments on the Timeline.

The **Events** feature shown as a tab on the previous page is used to publicise future fund-raising activities such as car boot sales. Facebook also allows extensive albums of photographs to be displayed, as shown below and discussed in more detail shortly.

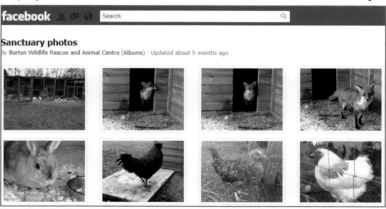

Facebook is an extremely powerful tool for informing the public about the work of the rescue centre and promoting future events. Also for receiving rapid feedback and offers of help.

Putting Your Photos on Facebook

Introduction

Earlier chapters have shown how you can include a photograph as part of your Facebook profile. The thumbnail version of this is used around the Facebook site so that your friends know they are looking at your pages and not those of someone else with the same name as you.

This chapter shows how the photos you take for pleasure or work can also be *uploaded* to Facebook. Chapter 8 describes the way *tags* can be used to identify people in photos. Photo albums and uploading videos to Facebook are also covered.

The Global Village

Facebook makes it extremely easy to post photographs and videos on your Home page and share them immediately with other people wherever they are in the world. This aspect of social networking can bring enormous benefits, such as:

- Viewing photos and videos of grandchildren who you might not otherwise be able to see growing up. Exchanging photos is also helpful in tracing family history.

- Swapping photos with friends or family of your hobbies, such as gardening or holidays.

- Posting videos explaining how to do tasks requiring skills, such as propagating plants or grafting fruit trees.

- Discussing images online with colleagues in other parts of the world in connection with business, employment or a profession, such as medicine, science or engineering.

Uploading Photos to Facebook

There are several ways of putting photos onto Facebook:

- Use a Webcam to take a photograph and use Facebook to upload it directly to your Facebook Web page.

- Locate photos already saved on your computer on the internal hard disc drive or on a removable device such as a flash drive (memory stick), CD or DVD, etc. Then use Facebook to upload them to the Facebook Web site.

Copying Photographs to Your Computer

Transferring photos to your computer's hard disc drive from a digital camera, or from a card reader or scanner is described in detail our book Computing and Digital Photography for the Older Generation (ISBN 978-0-85934-729-7) from Bernard Babani (publishing) Ltd.

Using a Webcam

Many new computers have an integral webcam, which takes the form of a small aperture built into the top of the monitor. Alternatively you can buy a separate webcam for just a few pounds. This usually has a long cable which plugs into one of the small rectangular USB ports on the front or back of the computer, as shown on the upper right. The cable allows you to move the camera about. For example, to take photographs outside in your garden, as shown at the bottom of the next page. Alternatively the webcam may be clipped to the top of a monitor as shown on the right, for example to take a photo for your Facebook profile.

To start using a webcam, select **Home** and **News Feed** and then click **Add photo/video** as shown below.

Now click **Use webcam** and the photo/video window opens as shown at the bottom of this page. An icon in the top right of the window allows you to switch between taking a photo and making a video. Click the circular radio button next to

Allow, on the **Settings** window as shown on the right above and then click **Close**. Click the blue camera icon (shown below) at the bottom of the window, to take the photo. There is a bar above the photo for you to write a short comment, replacing **Say something about this photo...** as shown below.

Sharing a Photograph

Now click the small downward arrow on the right of the audience selector icon near the bottom right of the screen and shown here on the right. This allows you to select the privacy for the photograph, such as

Friends. The **Custom** setting lets you make the photograph viewable by, or hidden from, specified people. When you click **Post** shown above, the photograph is posted on your Timeline and on your Home page under News Feed. It will also appear as a News Feed on your friends' Home pages, as shown below, where Jim has posted a photo on Jill's News Feed.

As shown above, your friends can write a **Comment** and also click **Lik**e to register their approval. A friend can also post the photo on their own Timeline if they wish.

Viewing Other People's Photographs

A photograph will be viewable by anyone who can see your Timeline; this depends on your privacy settings as discussed in Chapter 3, Protecting Your Privacy, starting on page 23.

For example, Stella can log in to Facebook and find Jim's Facebook pages using the search bar. Since Jim's privacy settings allow his posts to be viewed by everyone, Stella can see Jim's photos, even though she is not one of Jim's Facebook friends. In the example below, you can see that it is **Stella** who is logged in on this computer, since it is her name on the right-hand side of the blue Facebook bar. Having found Jim on Facebook by entering his name in the search bar, his Timeline, postings and photographs are fully visible to Stella. She simply clicks **Photos**, **Jim's Albums** and selects a particular album.

Photographs should be set to **Friends** as described below, to prevent people who are not your friends from seeing them.

Setting the Privacy on a Photo Album

To prevent Stella, or anyone else from seeing his photographs, Jim would need to go back to his **Home** page and select **Photos** and **My Albums**. Then from the drop-down menu obtained by clicking the audience selector icon, select **Friends**, as shown on the next page.

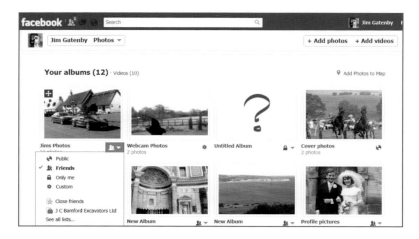

Uploading a Photo from Your Computer

Photographs stored on your computer's hard disc can easily be uploaded to the Facebook Web site. Photographs can also be uploaded from a removable medium such as a CD, DVD or *flash drive* (also known as a *memory stick*).

Photographs can easily be transferred from a digital camera to your hard disc prior to uploading to Facebook. Old photographic prints may be *scanned* and saved on the hard disc. (Please see note on page 74, **Copying Photographs to Your Computer**).

To upload a photo which is already stored on your computer, from your **Home** page select **News Feed**, click **Add photo/video** as shown below. Then select **Upload photo/video**.

A window opens up allowing you to start browsing or searching the folders on your computer for the required image.

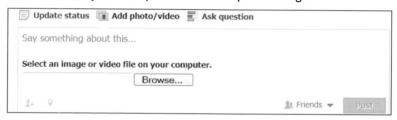

Photos Stored on the Hard Disc Drive

Click the **Browse...** button shown above and the **Choose File to Upload** window opens as shown below.

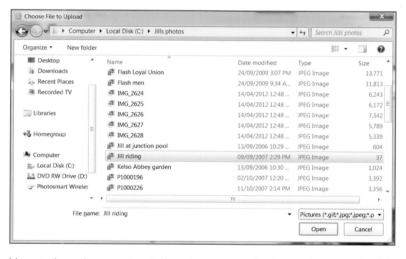

Now select the required disc drive, etc., folder and file and click the **Open** button, shown above. In this example, the file name of the photo is **Jill riding**, in a folder called **Jills photos** on the hard disc drive, **Local Disk (C:)** shown above. The next step is to set the privacy using the audience selector icon shown in the top image, before posting on Facebook, as discussed on page 81.

Photos On a Flash Drive or CD/DVD

If you have a photo saved on a removable device such as a flash drive (memory stick), the device will appear as something like **Removable Disk (E:)**, for example, as shown below on the left. Similarly a CD/DVD drive usually appears as drive **(D:)**.

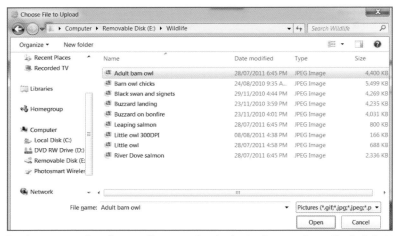

In the example above, the required photo image is called **Adult barn owl.JPG**, saved in a folder called **Wildlife** on a flash drive designated **Removable Disk (E:)**. When you click the **Open** button shown above, the full path name of the image **E:\Wildlife\Adult barn owl.JPG** appears on Facebook as shown below on the left of the **Browse...** button.

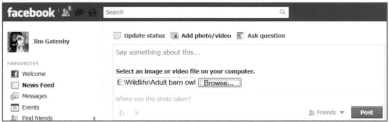

As shown above, there are bars in which you can type, if you wish to say something about the picture and where it was taken.

Sharing or Posting a Photograph

Having selected the required photograph, set the viewing audience such as **Friends**, for example, using the menu opened by clicking the audience selector icon shown on the right and at the bottom right of the screenshot below. Then click the **Post** button.

Within a minute or two the photo appears as an update on your News Feed on your Home page and also on your Timeline.

Depending on the privacy setting, the photo will also appear on the News Feed of people who are your Facebook friends. They can leave a comment, click **Like**, post it to their own Timeline or share it with a wider audience such as their own friends.

Enlarging a Photo Posted on Facebook

Clicking the small thumbnail image of the owl shown on the previous page displays the enlarged photo shown below.

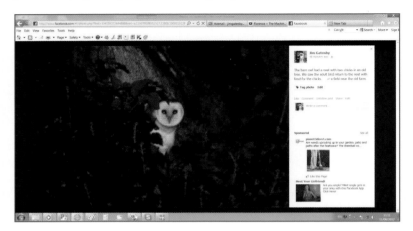

The panel shown on the right above allows you to write some notes about the photo, such as where it was taken and who you were with.

Facebook Photo Albums

Photographs which you upload to Facebook from your hard disc or other storage device are automatically saved in an album called **Wall Photos** created by Facebook. In Chapter 8 the creation of your own photo albums is discussed. This method is used when you are uploading a large number of photographs.

The JPEG Photographic File Format

You may have noticed the letters **.jpg** or **.JPG** at the end of the names of photo files, such as **Adult barn owl.JPG**. The **.jpg** file name extension is short for Joint Photographic Experts Group. This is a very common file format for photos saved on digital cameras, computers and on the Internet.

Tags, Albums and Videos

Introduction

The last chapter described the way photos can be uploaded to your Facebook pages from a computer or from a webcam. This chapter looks at the way photos can be *tagged* to identify the people in the image. Arranging photos in albums and the posting of videos to Facebook directly from a webcam are also discussed.

Tagging Photographs

If you have a photograph on Facebook which shows a group of people, tagging helps you to share the image with the people involved. When you tag a person in a photograph a connection is made with their Timeline on Facebook and they receive a notification saying that they have been tagged, including a copy of the photo. Anyone viewing a tagged photograph can pass their cursor over the people in the picture and see their names. In the example below a photograph from a family celebration was uploaded to Facebook from the hard disc drive as described in Chapter 7. A black menu bar along the bottom of the photo displays the various options, as shown below.

> **Tag photo**   **Options**   **Share**   **Like**

Click **Tag photo** on the black menu bar shown above. Then move the cursor over a person in the photograph and click the left mouse button. The menu of names shown on the right appears. Click the person's name if it is listed on the menu.

Otherwise type their name into the blank bar at the top of the menu. Repeat the process for the other people in the picture. Then click **Finished tagging** at the bottom right of the screen. Any of your friends tagged in the picture will receive a notification on their News Feed, saying that they have been tagged, together with a copy of the photograph, as shown below.

Clicking the photo displays the full size image. When a friend passes the cursor over each person in a photograph the person's name appears in a black rectangle as shown on the right, making it easy to identify everyone in a large gathering.

Photographs You Are Tagged In

Facebook allows you to view an album of all the photographs you are tagged in. You don't have to appear in a photo to be tagged in it — you can be tagged in a picture of a car, pet or a house, for example. Simply click anywhere over the photograph and enter your name as a tag, as described on page 83 and 84. The photos you are tagged in are automatically placed in a special area called **Photos of you**. This can be viewed by selecting **Home** from the right of the blue Facebook bar, then clicking **Photos** from the left-hand panel, before clicking **My Albums** towards the top right of the screen, as shown below.

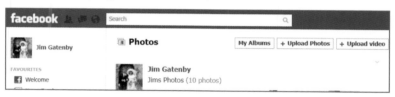

Then scroll down below the albums to the section **Photos of you** to see the photos you are tagged in, as shown below.

As shown in the top screenshot, the **Photos** section of your **Home** page has buttons **+Upload Photos** and **+Upload Video**. After clicking the appropriate button, browse your computer's storage devices such as the hard disc, flash drive or CD/DVD to locate the required photos before uploading them to Facebook.

Using Tags in Status Updates or Posts

You can include a tag in the text of a status update or post. This can make the update available to a wider audience. For example, if the audience selector is set at **Friends**, the post will be viewable by your friends plus the friends of anyone tagged in the post. This is the **Friends(+)** privacy setting shown below.

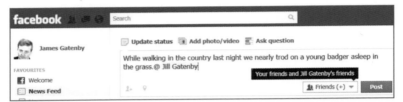

In the above example, James has posted an update and tagged Jill by inserting an **@** sign before her name. The update is posted on James' Home page and on his Timeline.

Jill receives a notification telling her she has been tagged. This can be viewed by clicking the Notification icon on the blue Facebook bar shown below, on the left of the Search bar.

The update is posted on Jill's Timeline as shown below. It is also posted on the Timelines of James' friends and Jill's friends

Anyone receiving this post can click on Jill's name and see her Timeline, as far as her privacy settings will allow. So if you post an update tagging the people you're with, other people can click the tagged names to find out about the people.

The icons in the top right-hand corner of the update, shown on the right are used to highlight or enlarge a post (left icon) or edit or delete one (right icon).

Adding Your Location to a Status Update or Post

An icon at the bottom of the status update window allows you to include your current location, as shown on the right, below on the left and near the top of page 86.

Click the icon, then type your location in the bar provided. Select your location from the drop-down menu which appears, such as **Bleaklow**, shown in the example below.

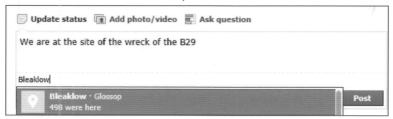

After you post the update, your friends will see your location in blue, as in Bleaklow, shown below. This is a clickable link which displays maps and information about your current location.

Creating Photograph Albums

From your **Home** page, select **News Feed** and click **Add photo/ video** and then **Create photo album**, as shown below.

This opens the **Select file(s)...** window shown below. First click the **Computer** icon shown on the right and below on the left. Then select the device on which the photos are stored. In the

example below, you can select a **DVD RW Drive (D:)**, a flash drive designated **Removable Disk (E:)**, in addition to the hard disc drive **OS(C:)**. The DVD drive can also read photos from an ordinary CD. Double-click first the device and then the required folder to display the photo files, as shown on the next page.

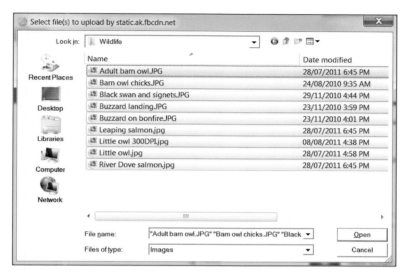

To select multiple photos, click the file name of each photograph while holding down the **Ctrl** key. Alternatively, to select a block of photos, hold down the **Shift** key and click the first and last file names. The selected files are highlighted in blue as shown above. They are also listed in the **File name** bar also shown above.

With the required files highlighted in blue, click **Open** and after a few seconds the photo album window opens and the process of uploading the photos to Facebook begins.

While the photos are being uploaded you can give a name to the photo album. You can set the resolution to high quality but this creates large files which are slow to handle. You can also set the privacy to **Public**, **Friends**, etc. There are spaces to type something about each picture and where it was taken. Finally click **Post photos** to share the photos with your friends or the audience you have selected with your privacy settings. The album now appears as a post on your Home page and on your Timeline, as shown on the next page.

Click on a thumbnail to enlarge the photo as shown below. There are options to edit the photograph and these are discussed in more detail shortly.

Viewing Your Photo Albums

Sign in to Facebook then select your **Home** page and click **Photos** and then **My Albums**.

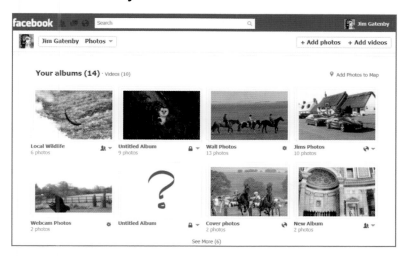

The **Webcam Photos** and **Cover Photos** albums shown above were created automatically when you upload pictures to your Timeline. Click an album as shown above to display the individual photographs, as shown below.

Editing a Photograph in an Album

When you click an individual photograph in an album, the image opens, filling most of the screen, as shown below.

At the bottom of the screen there are spaces to add a caption for the image and to write a comment.

By clicking the **Options** tag as shown on the right, you can rotate an image or download it from Facebook and save it as a file on your hard disc drive or a flash

drive (memory stick), etc. A further option allows you to *tag* the photograph as discussed earlier.

Putting Videos on Facebook

You can share videos with friends on Facebook. From your News Feed select **Add photo/video** as shown below. You can record your own video using a webcam or upload a video which has been saved on your hard disc drive as discussed shortly.

Recording a Video With a Webcam

For this option you need to have a webcam fitted to your computer. As discussed earlier, many new computers have a built-in webcam or you can buy a separate webcam on a cable that can be moved or clipped to your computer monitor. In order to watch videos you also need a piece of software called Adobe Flash Player installed. This is known as a *plugin* and works with a Web browser such as Internet Explorer or Mozilla Firefox. Adobe Flash Player can be downloaded for free from **www.adobe.com**.

If you have a separate webcam, make sure it's connected. Click **Use webcam** shown above, to open the webcam window shown below. An icon in the top right of the window allows you to switch between photo and video mode. Make sure video is selected. **Say something about this video...** should be displayed, as shown below.

A small window appears asking you to allow Facebook to access your camera and microphone. Click the radio button next to **Allow** and then click **Close**.

 Click the red button to start recording the video. Click the button again (now black) to stop recording.

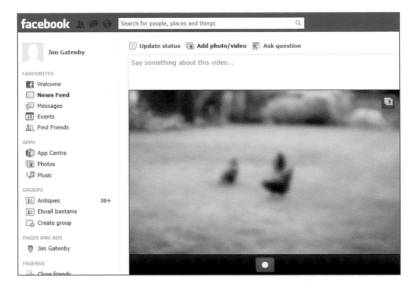

Enter a note in the box to replace the words **Say something about this video...** as shown above. Then use the audience selector to set the privacy (**Friends**, etc.) as discussed previously. Then click **Post** and the video is displayed on your Timeline and News Feed and on your friends' News Feeds according to your audience selector settings.

Your Video on a Friend's News Feed

Your friend receives a Notification about the video on the top left of the blue Facebook bar and a post of the video appears in their News Feed, as shown below. They can click the play the button shown below to start the video.

The video is played in a small window but can also be displayed full screen by clicking the button shown on the right and on the extreme right below. Press the Escape key to exit from full screen mode.

As shown above, there are buttons at the bottom of the window to pause the video and also mute or adjust the sound volume.

Deleting a Post

If you want to delete one of your posts such as an update, photo or video, click the cross on the right of the post then click the **Delete** button in the window which appears. The post is removed from your News Feed and Timeline and from your friends' News Feeds.

Videos Stored on Your Computer

This section describes the copying of a video which had previously been saved on your computer's hard disc drive. Transferring a photo or video to the Facebook Website on the Internet in this way is generally known as *uploading*.

The Windows Video Library

If you have Windows 7 you can easily practise this task using the sample videos stored in the video library. Click the Explorer icon on the Taskbar at the bottom of the screen, shown on the right and below.

Select **Libraries** from the left-hand side of the Explorer screen and then double-click the **Videos** icon as shown below.

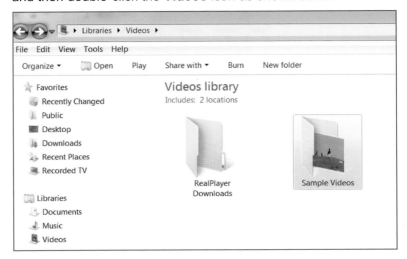

Double-click the **Sample Videos** folder shown above to see the icons for the stored videos such as the **Wildlife.wmv** video shown on the right.

Wildlife.wmv

Uploading a Video to Facebook

Now we know where the sample video is located on the hard disc drive, it's a simple job to upload it to Facebook. From your Home page select **Add photo/video** and **Upload photo/video** as shown on page 93.

Now click **Browse...** and locate the sample video in the appropriate folder as shown on the previous page. The video is called **Wildlife.wmv** and is stored in the **Sample Videos** folder in the **Videos Library**. Click the video file name and then click **Open** to place the full path name of the video on the left of **Browse...** shown below.

Now select the privacy level after clicking the audience selector icon, as shown above on the left of the word **Friends**.

Click **Post** to start the process of uploading the file to Facebook. As before, a notification including a thumbnail for the video appears on your Timeline and on your News Feed and your friends' News Feeds. Click the **Play** button to watch the video in an enlarged window or full screen.

Key Facts: Facebook Photos and Videos

- Photographs and videos are a major part of Facebook; your *profile photo* allows people who know you to recognise your pages on Facebook.

- Facebook enables millions of people to share their latest photos and videos with friends around the world.

- Facebook simplifies the process of *uploading* photos and videos from your computer to the Facebook Web site.

- Photographs can be uploaded from your hard disc drive or other storage medium such as a CD, DVD or flash drive.

- You can use a *webcam* to take a photo or video and upload it directly to Facebook.

- Your recent photographs appear on your Facebook *Timeline* and on your friends' *News Feeds*.

- Someone who is not your friend can find you on Facebook by searching for your name. The *audience selectors* should be used to control who can see your photos and videos, e.g. by using the Friends privacy setting.

- Photos can be organised into *albums*, each album containing up to 200 photographs.

- People appearing in a photograph can be *tagged* with their name. This provides a link to the person's Timeline with a notification that they have been tagged and includes a thumbnail of the photograph. People and places can be tagged in status updates as well as photos.

- Clicking a thumbnail displays an enlarged image; passing the cursor over a tagged photograph displays the names of any people who have been tagged.

- Short videos can be uploaded and viewed on Facebook in a similar way to still photographs.

More Facebook Features

Introduction

Previous chapters have covered the basic skills needed to get started with Facebook and how to use the main features. These include your Profile or Timeline, News Feed, Facebook Friends, and involve communication in various forms such as status updates, photos, videos and links to Web sites.

With these basic skills you should now be able to explore many other important features on Facebook such as those listed below and briefly described in the rest of this chapter.

- Facebook Mobile: Viewing your Facebook pages while on the move using a mobile phone.

- Apps: Software for various applications such as utilities for uploading photos and games and entertainment.

- Groups: Getting together online with other people to share information about a common interest.

- Notifications: Notes generated by Facebook informing you that something has happened on Facebook involving you.

- Networks: Facebook encompasses many networks based on schools, colleges and places of work. To join a network you need a valid e-mail address for the network.

- Events: Publicising forthcoming events with the place, date and time.

- Facebook Pages: special pages designed to promote a business, organisation, celebrity, cause or community.

Facebook on the Move

You can access Facebook from a mobile phone. With the latest Smartphones such as the iPhone or Blackberry (shown on the right) you can download a free Facebook App. This allows you to use miniature versions of most of the Facebook features available on a full-size  computer. The number of features you can use depends on the specification of your phone, as follows.

- If your phone can use SMS (Short Message Service) you can send and receive short text messages between Facebook and your mobile phone. These can be used to update your status or receive notifications.

- A mobile phone that can use MMS (Multi-media Message Service) can be used to upload photos and videos to Facebook.

- If your phone has a Web browser you can access the Facebook Mobile Web site at **http://m.facebook.com**, where you can use most of the Facebook features such as status updates, Timeline posts, News Feed and photos.

For help on setting up a mobile phone, from the **Home** menu select **Help**, **Visit the Help Centre**, **Facebook Basics** and **Use Mobile**. You can activate a mobile phone to receive Facebook text messages after clicking **Home**, **Account Settings** and then **Mobile** from the left-hand panel. These include notifications, messages, Wall posts and status updates.

Facebook Apps

These are applications, i.e. programs, which work within the Facebook environment. Some Apps are provided for free by Facebook itself while others are sold by third-party developers.

Click **Apps and Games** from the left-hand side of the Facebook Home page to open the window shown below. If you scroll downwards there are several screens listing apps and games. You can also display lists of **Recommended Games** and **Recommended Apps**.

One of the most popular Apps is the game called Farmville. This is a real-time simulation of farms, played by Facebook members or "neighbours" who can work together on joint farming activities. Starting off with an empty farm, neighbours grow crops and raise animals to earn as much money as possible.

FarmVille
Join your friends in FarmVille, the world's biggest farming game! Grow hundreds of crops, trees, and animals! More added every day
Olivia Kemps played FarmVille in the last month.

Before using a particular App you can choose either to allow the App to access your personal information or click a button to leave the App.

Facebook Groups

A group on Facebook is a page shared by a number of people with a common interest. You can join a group you're interested in or create a new group of your own. A group can have just a few members or several thousand.

For example, you might want to find out about any groups already up and running on a particular subject, such as antiques. Enter **antiques** in the Facebook search bar and at the bottom of the first short list of results, click **See more results for antiques**.

A longer list of results appears from which you now click **Groups** on the left-hand side of the screen, as shown below.

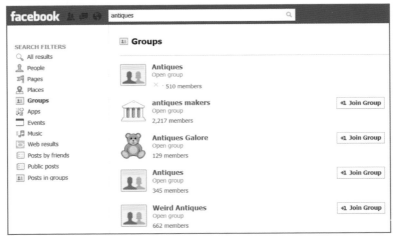

To find out about a particular group, click on its thumbnail picture as shown above. The Facebook page for the group opens as shown on the next page. The page for a group can include details and photographs of items for sale, such as antiques. Or members of the group might have a forum on a hobby such as gardening, where they can exchange ideas and discuss problems such as pests and diseases affecting plants. People are generally extremely willing to give such advice online.

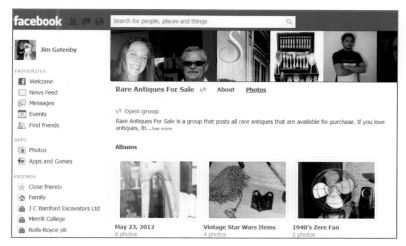

Three tabs shown above and below open up various pages giving information about this particular antiques group.

In this example, the tab **Rare Antiques for Sale** lists everything the group members wish to sell. **About** lists the members of the group, with links to their Timelines. **Photos** leads to numerous albums of photos of antiques.

The **Join group** button shown on the right sends a request for you to become a member of a group.

Creating a Group

From the left-hand panel on one of your Home pages, select **Create group**. Enter a name for the group and then enter the names of the people you want to be members. Then select either **Open**, **Closed** or **Secret** depending on the level of privacy you require for the group members and the information they post, as defined in the **Create New Group** window. Finally click the **Create** button to finish setting up the group..

Notifications

These are messages from Facebook, informing you of activity on Facebook that involves you. You can check your notifications by clicking the third blue icon on the right of the word **facebook**, as shown on the right and below. A small red  square appears on the blue bar, informing you of the number of new notifications.

Networks

To access a local area network supported by Facebook, you must have a valid e-mail address provided by the school, college or company, etc. To join a network, click **Account Settings** on the Home menu, then select **Networks** and enter the name of the network, your e-mail address and any other details required. Finally click the blue **Save Changes** button shown below.

Events

This feature allows you to publicise the details of any future gathering you are planning and to send out invitations. Shown below is an extract from the **Events** section of the Facebook page belonging to the Burton Wildlife Rescue and Animal Centre.

To create an event, from the left-hand side of your Home page click **Events** and then click **+ Create event** from the top right.

In the window shown below, enter the details of the event such as time and place. Then set the **Privacy** and click **Invite friends**. A window appears allowing you to select friends to invite to the event. Click **Save** and finally click **Create** shown below to complete the posting of the event details on Facebook..

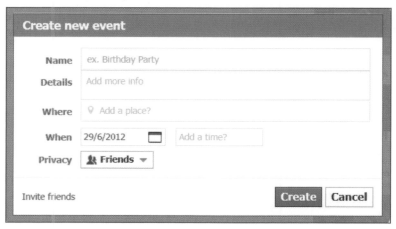

Pages for Businesses and Celebrities, etc.

You can set up a Facebook Page to promote a business, cause, or a celebrity, for example. On the initial Facebook Sign Up page, click **Create a Page for a celebrity, band or business**.

First select the type of organisation to be represented by the Page, such as a local business, a brand or product or an artist, band or public figure, or support for a cause. Then click on the appropriate icon shown below, choose a category and fill in your contact details before agreeing to the Facebook Pages Terms.

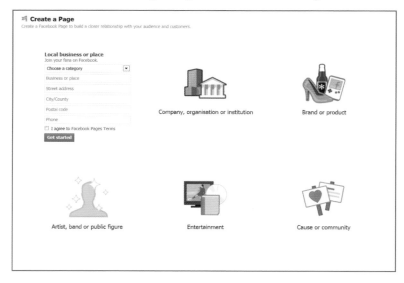

Now click **Get started** to begin building your Page. You will need to sign in to Facebook or create a new Facebook account. Then you can start uploading pictures, inserting information, links to Web sites and invitations for other people to participate.

A Glossary of Facebook Terms

Applications   Usually known as *Apps* for short, these are programs on Facebook such as games and software for uploading photographs.

Audience Selectors   Icons and menus used to control who can see your information. (Privacy settings).

Chat   This facility allows you to have a real-time conversation with friends by typing the words into a small window on the screen.

Comment   This enables you to type a short note in response to a status update or photograph.

Events   This feature allows you to inform friends about future events and social occasions.

Facebook   A worldwide social network with over 900 million members, exchanging news and information, photographs and videos.

Friend   A person with whom you have agreed to exchange information on Facebook.

Friend request   An offer of friendship on Facebook which can be either accepted or declined.

Group   This feature allows Facebook users to collaborate with other people sharing a common interest and to join online forums.

Home page   The Home page contains your News Feed and links to many other features such as Messages, Events and Friends.

Like   Clicking the word *Like* is a quick way to register your approval of an update or photo.

Message   A note sent to a particular friend or friends, similar to an e-mail. May include photos, etc.

News Feed   Part of your Home page, informing you of your friends' latest activities on Facebook.

Notifications	These are short messages which pop up on the screen telling you about something that happened on Facebook.
Page	Page in this context refers to a special feature for businesses, organisations, bands and celebrities, etc., to broadcast information to a wide audience.
Poke	This is a way of saying hello to a friend and reminding them you exist and are online.
Post	A status update, photo or video placed on your or your friends' Walls or News Feeds.
Privacy Settings	Audience selector settings used to control who can see which parts of your Facebook information and photographs, etc.
Profile	Your Profile (Timeline) lists your personal information, photos, career and interests as well as posts stating what you've been doing.
Status	A short update to friends saying what you're doing or what's on your mind. A photo, video or Web link can be attached. Friends can reply by writing a comment or clicking *Like*.
Tagging	Labelling a friend's name on a photo, sending an update and the photo to the friend's Wall.
Timeline	A listing of all your personal information (your Profile) and your activities on Facebook, listed in chronological order including photos, status updates and posts from your friends.
Wall	Part of your Timeline where you can post updates, photos, videos, etc.
Webcam	A small camera which plugs into a USB port on a computer or which is built into a screen. Used to take profile photos or pictures of objects close to the computer.

Introducing Twitter

What is Twitter?

These days you can't watch television, listen to the radio or read a newspaper without Twitter being mentioned. This chapter gives an overview of Twitter and what it's used for. Subsequent chapters give more detailed instructions about setting up a Twitter account and how to use it.

Like Facebook, Twitter is a social network, allowing people to communicate and interact over the Internet. Twitter is the second most popular social network behind Facebook and has millions of users posting hundreds of millions of *tweets* a day.

What is a Tweet?

As shown below, a tweet is a short text message which can be immediately viewed by an audience of thousands or even millions of people — if you're a celebrity or well-known person.

james gatenby @jimgatenby   9h
For once the sun is shining, the birds are singing and everything in the garden is rosy - but for how long?
Expand ← Reply 🗑 Delete ★ Favorite

Lots of ordinary people use Twitter to tell their friends and families what is happening in their lives. Many Web sites representing companies and organisations include a link to their Twitter pages

Latest News

where you can read their latest news. Celebrities and people with a lot of interested followers can use Twitter to get their message out to a wide audience. Twitter can also be used to host a debate or to marshal support for a charitable cause.

Some of the essential features of Twitter are:

- Tweets, i.e. messages, can be up to 140 characters long.
- Tweets are posted onto the Home page of *followers*.
- Apart from text, a tweet can include a link to a photograph, video or a Web site.

The 140 Character Tweet Limit

The SMS text messages used on mobile phones were an influence on the creators of Twitter. It was thought that by enforcing a limit of 140 characters, "Tweeters" would be more concise and organise their thoughts better — "brevity is the soul of wit". If you try to enter more than 140 characters, the message is truncated. You don't have to use the full 140 characters if you don't need to. The number **33** next to the **Tweet** button below is the number of characters available before the limit is reached. **What's happening?** shown below is only a rough guide to the contents of a Tweet, which can be anything you like as long as it's not offensive. In that case the Tweet may be removed.

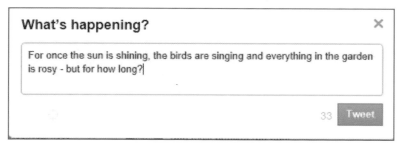

The Tweet appears on your Home page and on the Home pages of the people following you. Creating a Tweet can include the insertion of links to photographs, videos and Web sites. These topics are discussed in more detail in Chapter 13.

Followers

Twitter is based on the concept of *followers.* A follower is someone who is interested in reading someone else's Tweets. Although celebrities can have millions of followers, you could equally have a small group of friends or relatives following each other. When you post a Tweet it appears almost immediately on the Home pages of all your followers. A link at the bottom of a Tweet allows followers to post a reply. The followers of important people or celebrities may simply want to read the Tweets out of interest, without expecting to take part in a two way conversation.

In the case of a small group of friends or family communicating on Twitter, you post an immediate reply. You can also *Retweet* or forward someone else's Tweet to the people following you.

Normally when you post a Tweet, anyone can see it after searching for your name. It's possible to set the privacy so only your approved followers can see the Tweet, as discussed later.

Twitter allows you to search for people by name or by their e-mail address and then start following them or you can invite friends to join Twitter via e-mail. Twitter also displays a list of celebrities you may wish to follow. You can choose who you want to follow, but you can't choose who follows you. You can *unfollow* someone you no longer wish to follow.

Direct Messages

Normally when you create a Tweet it is sent to all of the people who are following you. *Direct messages* are sent to a particular person who is following you.

Direct Messages are discussed in more detail in Chapter 13.

Twitter and Photos

A Tweet can include a link to a file such as a photograph, as shown below. You can also insert links to videos and Web sites.

Clicking either the blue link **View photo** or the link **pic.twitter...** above opens the image, as shown below.

Inserting links into Tweets is discussed in detail in Chapter 13.

Profile Information

As discussed in more detail later, you can create a *Profile* for yourself or your business.

The profile information appears along the top of the Twitter page as shown above and can include a photo or image, up to 700KB in size. Up to 160 characters of text are allowed, a location to say where you are and a link to a Web site. In the example above, a Twitter account had recently been set up for my publisher, Babani Books of London. Tweets on the right-hand side give news of the latest books (including this one). The blue text at the end of each Tweet represents clickable links which open up large size photos of each book cover. The profile page also displays thumbnail images of photos that you have recently posted on Twitter.

Creating and editing your Profile is discussed in more detail in Chapter 14.

The Twitter Search Bar

You can look at all the Tweets on a particular subject by entering the key word(s) in the Twitter Search bar across the top of the screen. Topical subjects such as **climate change**, **Wimbledon** or **floods**, for example all yield large numbers of the very latest Tweets.

Hashtags

This is a hash symbol (**#**) you can place in front of an important keyword anywhere in a Tweet, as in the *#floods* example below. If readers of the message click over the hashtag, all other Tweets on the same subject are displayed.

Getting Help on Twitter

 There is a lot of useful help built into Twitter. This can be displayed after clicking the small downward pointing arrow on the right of the *person icon* shown above on the left. Then select **Help** from the menu shown on the right.

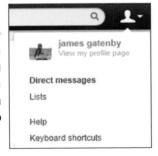

Some Uses of Twitter

- Share latest news and information with friends and family in a two-way "conversation" based on Tweets, i.e. 140 character text messages.

- Send Tweets including photos and videos of friends and family, special occasions, etc. Also links to Web sites.

- *Retweet*, i.e. forwarding Tweets you have received to other people who you think might be interested.

- If you have a large number of followers you can ask questions and receive a lot of helpful answers.

- Enlist support for a good cause or charitable event.

- Exchange views with many other people in an online debate about a current "hot" topic or *trend*.

- People who are interested in a particular person, business or celebrity can become a Twitter *follower* and receive all their latest thoughts, news and ideas.

- You can find out when a celebrity, public figure, etc., who you are following is appearing in your area, etc.

- A business can use Twitter for all its latest news flashes. For example, newspapers can give breaking news in a Tweet, with a link to the full story on their Web site.

- A retailer such as a food outlet, e.g., butcher, farm shop, restaurant, etc., can quickly list all their latest seasonal offers and include clickable links to photographs. Faster and more up-to date than newspaper advertising.

- Organisations can post Tweets such as flood or severe weather warnings, which can easily be found using the Twitter Search feature or hashtags.

- The Web site flightradar24.com monitors flights in real time and uses Twitter to post emergency alerts.

Before You Start Using Twitter

This book has been prepared using laptop and desktop PC computers. If you're going to use Twitter on the move then you can also use one of the latest tablet computers such as the iPad or a *smartphone* such as a Blackberry or iPhone.

As discussed in the next chapter you can connect to Twitter after entering the Twitter Web address shown below. This can also be achieved using the built-in Web browser on a smartphone.

www.twitter.com

You are then asked to sign in or sign up to Twitter, as discussed in detail in the next chapter. Using Twitter is free to the ordinary user, although you might run up some charges on a smartphone as a result of your Twitter usage. Smartphones like the iPhone and Blackberry also have their own Apps used to run Twitter.

Twitter, unlike Facebook, doesn't stipulate a minimum age of membership, or ask for your age or sex. The only thing you need is an e-mail address and a connection to the Internet.

Promoted Tweets

Although free to individual users, Twitter charges companies to advertise using *Promoted Tweets*. These are similar to normal Tweets, but are marked to show that they are being used for promotional purposes. Twitter targets Promoted Tweets at users whose activities on Twitter suggest they'll be interested in the products or services being advertised. Promoted Tweets are marked Promoted by... and appear at the top of the list of results after a search on Twitter.

Chapter 11 gives step-by-step instructions for signing up and starting to use Twitter.

Getting Started With Twitter

Signing Up

All you need to create your own Twitter account is a computer connected to the Internet and a genuine e-mail address. If you haven't got your own e-mail address you could sign up for a Windows Live ID at **http://uk.msn.com**. The Windows Live ID acts as a passport to various Windows programs such as the new Outlook.com e-mail program (replacing Hotmail) and Windows Live Messenger, used for instant messaging and video calling. Outlok.com and Windows Live Messenger are discussed in Chapter 15.

Your new e-mail address would then be something like:

johnsmith@live.co.uk

Now on your Web bowser such as Internet Explorer or Mozilla Firefox, enter the address of the Twitter Web site.

The following window opens, allowing existing users of Twitter to **Sign in** and **New to Twitter** users to **Sign up**.

After entering your full name, e-mail address and password, Twitter reports on your details and assigns a **Username** to you, based on your e-mail address. If a name has already been used Twitter suggests other usernames based on your own name or adds a digit to your name as in **StellaAustin7**, for example. It also comments on the security of your password, which in this case could be improved by adding some numbers..

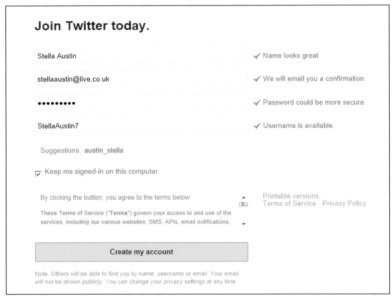

You are then advised to read the terms of service and if you are happy with them, click **Create my account** to get started.

You may then be required to complete the short *CAPTCHA* test by typing in the two words to prove you are human. The distorted letters in the CAPTCHA are meant to be impossible for a computer program to read. This is designed to prevent malicious automated software trying to damage a service like Twitter by bombarding it with false applications to create accounts. This might slow the Twitter service down, making it unusable.

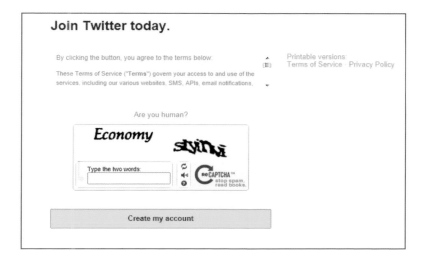

Now click **Create my account** again. This opens the following window, with a **Welcome** message and help from **The Twitter Teacher**.

When you click **Next** you are given the chance to start following people and reading their Tweets. Twitter suggests that you start following five people initially from the list in the left hand panel. Click the grey **Follow** button displaying the Twitter bird logo shown on the right and on the next page.

After clicking a **Follow** button it changes to the blue **Following** button as shown on the right and on the next page. Tweets posted by the people you have chosen to follow appear in the right-hand panel.

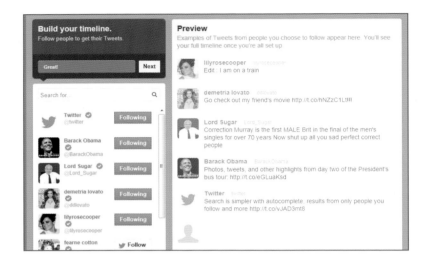

After clicking **Next** you are presented with the following screen which allows you to search your e-mail contacts.

If you select an e-mail service you are asked to sign in to the service. Twitter asks for your permission to search the contacts list. If they are already on Twitter you can click the **Follow** button to follow them, as shown on the next page. Otherwise Twitter will send them an e-mail inviting them to join.

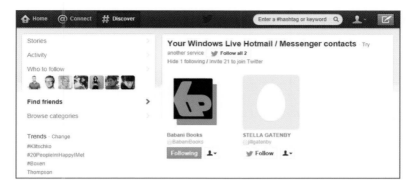

During the sign up process you are given the chance to enter the information for your Twitter Profile.

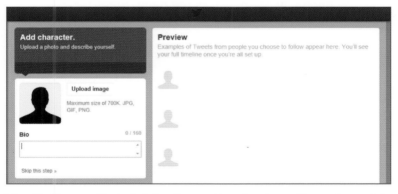

The Twitter profile is briefer than a Facebook profile and consists of up to 160 characters of biographical information plus a photo, logo or image, etc. A profile photo must be no more than 700k (kilobytes). Many photos taken on a digital camera are much bigger than this, so you may need to reduce the size of your image using a program like Adobe Photoshop Elements, as discussed elsewhere in this book. If you wish you can click this step and complete your Profile later using **Edit your profile**, as discussed in detail in Chapter 14.

A Tour of Twitter

Twitter is operated by the black menu bar across the top of the screen, as shown in the extract below.

Clicking **Home**, shown above, opens your Home page, containing your Timeline and all the Tweets posted by you or by the people you are following, as shown below.

After the initial sign up process you should have selected a few of the suggested people or organisations to follow. As shown below on the top left of Stella' Home page, Stella has chosen to follow 10 people. She has not yet sent any Tweets and no one is following her.

In fact you don't need to have any followers yourself, or send any Tweets. You might just use Twitter in a passive way, by reading the Tweets of people or organisations that interest you. However, if you want to use Twitter to have a continuing dialogue with friends and family, you will need to follow each other, as discussed shortly

The lower left-hand panel on the Home page lists more people you may wish to follow. You can also click **Browse categories** to look through various categories such as sport, music and entertainment to find people to follow.

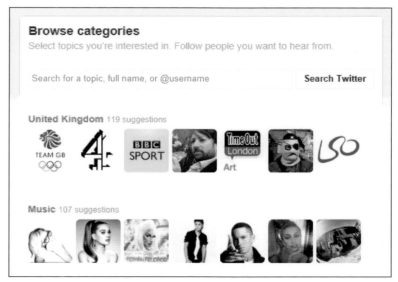

When you have selected a person or organisation which interests you, click the **Follow** button, as shown below.

Now whenever this person or organisation posts a Tweet, it will appear in the right-hand panel of your Home page.

The Timeline

The right-hand panel on your Twitter Home page is your *Timeline*. This is a long list of Tweets, with the latest Tweets at the top. This lists all the Tweets from the people you are following. It also displays the Tweets you post yourself. As shown on the screenshot below, on the right of each Tweet is the length of time since the Tweet was posted. On the left of the Tweet is the Profile picture, typically a photograph or a logo.

@Connect

Clicking this tab on the left of the menu bar lists the people who have interacted with you on Twitter, such as becoming one of your followers.

Clicking **Mentions** above lists all the Tweets which have included your username, such as **@johnsmith**.

#Discover

Clicking this tab displays a menu of several Twitter features, as shown in the left-hand panel below.

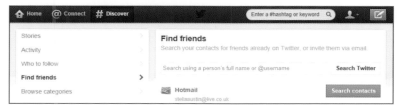

Stories

These are the latest news headlines, with links to Web sites and videos, etc.

Activity

This shows what the people you are following are doing on Twitter such as the people they are following and the Tweets they have marked as their *favorites*.

Who to follow

This displays a list of well-known people who you may wish to follow on twitter by clicking the **Follow** buttons shown on the right below.

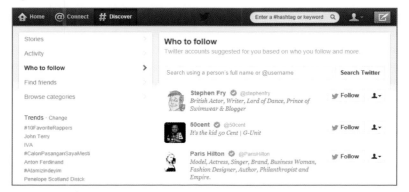

Find Friends

This option is shown below in the left-hand panel, displayed after clicking the **#Discover** tab on the Twitter menu bar. With this option you can search for friends already on Twitter by entering their full name or Twitter name in **Search Twitter** shown below.

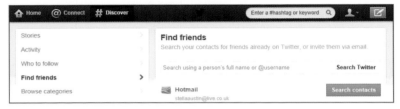

As shown below, you can also search your e-mail contacts lists to find people who are already on Twitter.

E-mail contacts not already on Twitter may be sent an invitation to join the social network after entering their e-mail addresses in the bar shown below, and clicking **Invite friends**.

Once you've found friends on Twitter, click **Follow**. If you and your friends are following each other, you will be able to have a two-way conversation, as discussed in more detail shortly.

Browsing Categories

This option allows you to look at people you may wish to follow by browsing through lists of suggestions, in categories such as music and sport. When you click a person or organisation which interests you, you are presented with a button to click to **Follow** them.

This option may also appear in the left-hand panel of your Home page, as discussed in more detail on page 123.

Twitter also has a lot of recommendations of its own for you to follow, such as **Top Tweets**, shown below.

Click the **Follow** button to start receiving the Tweets of a person or organisation that interest you.

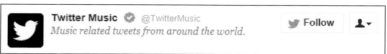

The Twitter Search Bar

This is situated on the right-hand side of the Twitter menu bar as shown below.

You simply type in a *#hashtag* such as **#wimbledon** to find all the Tweets on that topic. As discussed in Chapter 10, a #hashtag is a link to all the Tweets on a popular topic. On clicking the magnifying glass icon (or pressing the Enter key) the search   produces a list of Tweets about Wimbledon in the right-hand panel as shown in the extract below.

The left-hand panel displays links to people, videos and images relating to the Wimbledon championships.

A *keyword* search might be useful if you wanted to find out what other people had to say about an obscure subject, such as **quantitive easing** for example. Just enter the keywords in the Twitter search bar to obtain a list of relevant Tweets with clickable links to Web sites, videos, etc.

Clicking the *person icon* shown on the right and below displays the following drop-down menu.

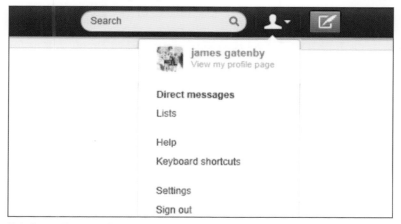

Brief outlines of the above options are given below. More detailed descriptions are given elsewhere in this book.

View my profile page shown at the top of the above menu displays the Tweets you have posted, your biographical details and any photographs you have recently posted.

Direct messages are messages sent to one of your followers, rather than to all of your followers, as in the case of a Tweet.

Lists are described on pages 138 and 139.

Help opens the comprehensive Twitter Help Center, including answers to frequently asked questions and the Twitter Glossary.

Keyboard shortcuts enable certain operations to be carried out using designated key presses rather than using a mouse, e.g. for people who are fast typists or find a mouse difficult to use.

Settings are described in Chapter 14 and include details of your Twitter account, your background design and the ways you interact with Twitter. Apps or programs which can access your account are also listed and there is an option to edit your Profile.

Sign out closes your current connection to the Twitter Web site.

Composing a New Tweet

Whenever you want to post a new Tweet click the quill icon on the right of the Twitter menu bar, as shown on the right and below. The

What's happening? window opens as shown below ready for you to start typing in a Tweet.

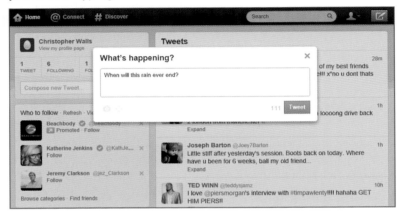

As you type, the Tweet button changes to blue as shown above. The number of characters available to be used is displayed near the bottom right, after being initially set at the maximum of 140. If you exceed 140 characters, a negative number is displayed and your message is cut down to 140 characters.

Two faint icons at the bottom left of the screen allow you to add a link to a photograph and also give your current location, as discussed later.

As shown above, it's easy to send a Tweet. However, unless you have some followers, no-one will see the Tweet apart from your self. Friends and relatives who wish to use Twitter for two-way conversations therefore need to agree to follow each other.

The next chapter shows how friends and relatives can communicate easily using Twitter.

Following Friends and Family on Twitter

Introduction

The last chapter described how you can sign up to Twitter and select people or organisations to follow from categories presented by Twitter. Then whenever they post a Tweet, you will receive a copy of the Tweet in your Timeline, the right-hand panel of your Twitter Home page. This automatically shows all the Tweets posted by the people you are following. It also shows the Tweets you have posted.

Of course, there is no point in posting a Tweet if you haven't got any followers — it will only appear on your Timeline and no-one else's. Someone who is not following you might, if they were sufficiently interested, find you on Twitter by doing a search using your name. Then they could see your Tweets. It is possible to prevent this by altering the *privacy* of your Tweets to change the possible viewing audience from *public* (everyone has access) to *approved followers only*. These *protected Tweets* are discussed in Chapter 14.

Many people may be happy just to read the Tweets of prominent people and organisations that interest them, without actually posting any Tweets of their own. You can reply to a Tweet posted by a celebrity but with so many followers they probably won't reply. However, if you want to have an online conversation with friends or family, you need to arrange to be following each other. Then you will automatically see each other's Tweets in your Timeline as soon as they are posted.

The next few pages show how two new users of Twitter can arrange to be followers of each other to exchange Tweets. The same methods can be used for larger groups of friends or family.

Tweets Between Friends and Family

A group of friends or family members can have an on going conversation by exchanging Tweets on Twitter no matter where they live in the world. They can see each other's Tweets as soon as they are posted. However, in order for someone to receive your Tweets they must be following you. You can choose to follow someone else but you can't make someone follow you. You must persuade or invite them to follow you, perhaps by sending them an e-mail, as discussed in Chapter 11.

In the following example, two relatives, Stella Austin and Christopher Walls have already got their own e-mail accounts. They have also created Twitter accounts as described in Chapter 11. When creating their usernames, Christopher and Stella found that other people had already used their names as *usernames*, so they accepted Twitter's suggested usernames of **christowalls** and **StellaAustin7**.

In order for two people to start exchanging Tweets, both need to:

- Sign in to Twitter.
- Use **Find friends** to search Twitter for the other person.
- Click the **Follow** button.

Signing in to Twitter

First start Twitter by entering **www.twitter.com** in the Address Bar of your Web browser such as Internet Explorer or Mozilla Firefox. Alternatively you can double-click an icon on your Windows Desktop, as discussed in Chapter 14.

Please Note: You *Sign up* to create a new Twitter user account. You *Sign in* at the start of every Tweeting session.

Enter your username or e-mail address in the **Sign In** bar, followed by your password, as shown at the bottom of the previous page. On clicking **Sign in**, Stella's Home page opens, as shown below. The lower left-hand panel shows Twitter's suggestions of more celebrities to follow. The right-hand panel shows the latest Tweets from the people Stella is already following.

As this is a brand new Twitter account, the top left-hand panel shows that Stella has not yet sent any Tweets. She is following 8 people or organisations out of those suggested to her by Twitter

during the sign up process, as discussed in Chapter 11. Currently Stella has not got any followers to read any Tweets she posted, but this is soon to be rectified. Stella chose to skip entering a photo for her profile page during the sign up process. That is why the small, egg-shaped icon appears next to her name. You can edit your Profile at any time, including your profile photograph and biographical details, as discussed in Chapter 14.

Finding and Following Friends or Family

Stella and Christopher want to exchange Tweets, so they must become followers of each other. You can find someone to follow by entering their username in the Search Bar at the top of the page, as shown below when Stella enters Christopher's username.

It's better to enter the unique username suggested by Twitter here, if you know it, otherwise you may need to find them in a long list of people with the same name.

You then have a choice of selecting **Tweets** or **People** on the upper left-hand panels shown above. Click **People** and then click the **Follow** button to start following them, as shown on the right.

As shown above, the **Follow** button changes to **Following** against a blue background.

Note from the above search, a person who is not following you can find you as a result of a search and see your Tweets unless you make them *protected*, i.e. only viewable by approved followers, as discussed in Chapter 14.

Another approach is to start by clicking **Find friends**, in blue on the left-hand side of the Home page under **Who to follow,** as shown here on the right. Alternatively click **#Discover** on the menu bar across the top of the screen then select **Find friends**.

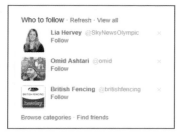

As discussed previously, this allows you to search for people using their full name, username or e-mail address. If not already on Twitter, they can be sent an e-mail inviting them to join.

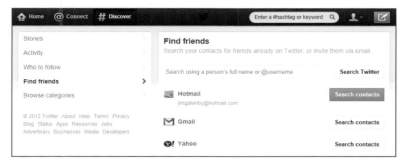

In the example on the previous page, Stella has become a follower of Christopher after finding him on Twitter using a search based on his username. In the same way, Christopher can do a search for Stella, as shown below.

Then select **People** and click **Follow** to start following Stella.

Stop Following (Unfollow) on Twitter

If you no longer want to receive the Tweets of someone you have been following, you can *unfollow* them. Sign in to Twitter and from your Home page, click **Following** and the right-hand panel should now show a list of the people you are following, as shown below.

Against all of the people or organisations you are following, there is a blue **Following** button. If you hover the cursor over the **Following** button it should change to **Unfollow** against a  red background. Click the button to remove the person or organisation from the list of people you are following.

When you click to **Unfollow** a person you've been following, their Tweets are deleted from your Timeline. You may need to click **View** and **Refresh** to make the Tweets disappear straightaway.

Blocking Someone from Following You

Christopher Walls has one follower, Stella Austin. He wants to prevent her from seeing his postings. You can't choose who follows you, but you can *block* a follower so they can't see your Tweets. First Christopher signs in to Twitter and from his Home page selects **Followers**.

From the list of followers (only one in this example) he selects the person he wishes to block (Stella) and clicks the icon next to **Follow** to display the drop down menu. From this Christopher selects **Block@StellaAustin7** as shown above.

Now Stella will no longer receive Christopher's Tweets on her Home page Timeline.

Please note: In the two above screenshots, Twitter has inserted standard icons, shown on the right, because Christopher and Stella have not yet inserted their own Profile photographs. This is discussed in detail Chapter 14.

Unblocking a Follower

If Christopher decides to allow Stella to start receiving his Tweets again on her Home page, he can unblock her. First he signs in to Twitter as himself. Then he searches for Stella by entering her username in the search bar at the top of the screen. Then from the search results screen he clicks Stella's name to show her Profile page as shown below.

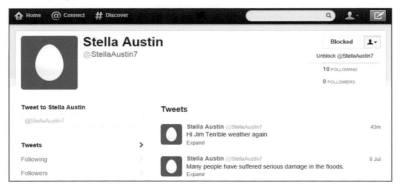

If Christopher clicks the head and shoulders icon, the option to unblock Stella is displayed, as shown on the right and above right. When Christopher clicks **Unblock**,

the **Blocked** button changes to **Follow** and this can be clicked to change it back to display **Following** against a blue background.

Lists

A *list* is a group of Twitter users whose Tweets you wish to follow in a single stream. Clicking to view a list displays all of the Tweets for the people on the list. For example, you could make a list of all your favourite football teams. When you click the list's name, the latest Tweets from all of the teams are displayed.

Alternatively, a list could be a group of your friends or family or members of a club.

Creating a List

From your Home page, select **View my profile** page and then select **Lists** and **Create List** as shown on the right. Enter a name and a description for the list and click **Save list**.

You are then presented with a search bar allowing you to search for a Twitter user to add to the list, e.g. **Arsenal**. From the search results shown below, click the person icon (head and shoulders) and then **Add or remove from lists...**, as shown below.

A window opens allowing you to tick the required list. Now search for the rest of the Twitter users to be included on the list and add them to the list in the same way.

Viewing a List

From your Profile page, select **Lists** and click the name of the list you want to view. All of the Tweets for the people or organisations in the list are displayed as shown below.

Key Facts: Following on Twitter

- You can follow anyone you like on Twitter.
- Twitter displays lists of people and organisations which you can choose to follow.
- You can find people and follow them by entering their name in the Twitter search bar. Then click **Follow**.
- The Tweets of people you follow appear on your *Timeline* on the right of your Home page.
- You cannot choose who follows you.
- If you want someone to follow you so that you can exchange Tweets, you must become mutual followers.
- You might invite people to follow you, e.g. by e-mail, on your correspondence, stationery or Web site, etc.
- You can stop following someone by hovering over the **Follow** button and clicking **Unfollow** when it appears.
- When you unfollow someone, their Tweets are removed from your Timeline.
- People who are not following you may see your Tweets after entering your name in the Twitter search bar.
- You can *Protect* your Tweets so that only your approved followers can see them.
- The *Block* option allows you to stop one of your followers from seeing your Tweets. If you change your mind there is an *Unblock* option.
- You can create *Lists* of your followers making it easy to display the Tweets of particular groups of people or organisations.
- Clicking a follower's name at the top of a Tweet displays their Profile page.

13

Posting and Receiving Tweets

Posting a New Tweet

Now Stella and Christopher are following each other they can start tweeting and they know that at least one other person will see their Tweets. Stella signs in and types her

message into **Compose new Tweet** on the left-hand panel. Alternatively you can select the **Compose new Tweet** icon on the right of the Twitter menu bar, as shown above.

After typing her message, Stella clicks the Tweet button at the bottom right of the new Tweet window, as shown on the right. The

Tweet immediately appears on Stella's own Timeline and on the Timelines of anybody following her. (At this stage only Christopher is following Stella).

Similarly Christopher can sign in and type a Tweet. When he clicks the Tweet button his message will appear on his Timeline and the Timeline of anybody following him. The faint icons on the bottom left of the window shown on the right are used to include a *photograph* with a Tweet and to give your *location*, as discussed shortly.

The same Tweets appear on both Stella's and Christopher's Timelines in chronological order of Tweeting, with the latest Tweets on top, as shown below. Each Tweet is headed by the Tweeter's full name followed by their Twitter username.

Stella's Home Page

Christopher's Home Page

Obviously this was a very simple example involving only two people, but the same methods can be used for a much larger group of friends, family or colleagues in an organisation. Since you can't make someone follow you, you may need to persuade them or invite them by e-mail to follow you. Many companies have a link on their Web site to a Twitter **Follow** button or there may be notes on stationery and advertisements.

Tweeting is very fast, so if several followers are simultaneously online they can have a conversation effectively in real time.

Responding to Tweets

Once you start following people on Twitter, their Tweets will start appearing on the Timeline on your Home page, along with the Tweets you have posted. After reading a Tweet, there are many ways you can respond to it.

- Post a *reply*
- *Retweet* it to all of your followers
- Mark it as a *favorite* for viewing later and to tell the original Tweeter that you liked their Tweet.
- Click on a *hashtag* (e.g. *#climate*) within a Tweet to find other Tweets on the same topic as the hashtag.

When you click **Expand** below a Tweet as shown on the right, some further options appear, as shown below on the right of **Collapse**.

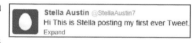

The top Tweet was posted by Christopher on his own Timeline and includes options to **Reply**, **Delete** and mark the Tweet as a **Favorite**. The lower Tweet, posted by Stella on Christopher's Timeline has options to **Reply**, **Retweet** and mark as **Favorite**.

Replying to a Tweet

Christopher received from Stella the Tweet shown below.

He clicks **Expand** at the bottom of the Tweet as shown on page 142 and 143 to display the **Collapse**, **Reply**, **Retweet** and **Favorite** options, shown above. If Christopher clicks **Reply**, the following window opens up. The username of the sender of the original message, i.e. **@StellaAustin7** is inserted automatically at the start of the reply and across the top after **Reply to…**.

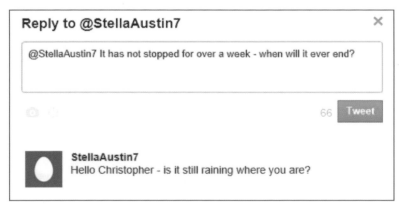

Christopher posts the reply by clicking **Tweet** shown above. Both the original Tweet from Stella and the reply from Christopher appear on both of their Timelines.

Other people will only see a reply if they are following both the sender and the recipient of the reply.

The original Tweet from Stella and the reply from Christopher are shown below in Stella's Timeline.

If Stella clicks **View conversation**, the order of the two Tweets is reversed, making the conversation easier to read.

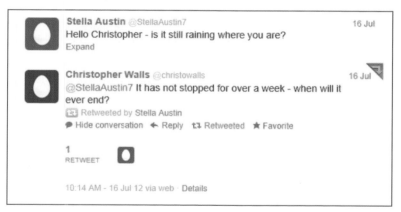

If you have a reply in your Timeline and you are not sure what Tweet it's replying to, hover over the Tweet to highlight it. If you now click the Tweet, the original Tweet is displayed above the reply, as shown above.

A reply starts with the username of the person who posted the original Tweet, as in "**@StellaAustin7 It has not stopped**..." as shown above.

Retweeting

This is similar to forwarding an e-mail message. If you receive a Tweet from someone you are following, the Retweet option sends a copy of the Tweet to all of your followers. Click **Retweet** at the bottom of a Tweet, as shown on pages 143 and 144 and the following window opens.

In the example below, Stella's original message has been Retweeted by Christopher to all of his followers.

The note **Retweeted by Christopher Walls** appears on the Tweet when it is read by Christopher's followers.

In Christopher's Timeline a small arrow against a green background is placed in the top right-hand corner of his own copy of the message he has Retweeted.

RT@username

A Retweet can also be sent using the New Tweet box. Type **RT@username**, e.g. **RT@christowalls**, then type in or copy and paste in the original message. This gives credit to the original Tweeter and you can add text of your own up to 140 characters. Click **Tweet** to Retweet the message to all your followers.

Editing and Deleting Tweets

You can't edit a Tweet. If you make a mistake you could delete the erroneous version and send a new, corrected version, perhaps with a covering note if there is room.

As the screenshot above is part of Christopher's Timeline, there is only a **Delete** option on the Reply he had posted.

Alternatively click **View my profile page** at the top left of your Home page. This shows just the Tweets you have posted. Click **Expand** on the Tweet to display the **Delete** option. Click **Delete** and **Yes** to remove the Tweet from your Timeline. You can only delete

Tweets one at a time, as described above. If you stop following someone, as discussed on page 136, all their Tweets are removed from your Timeline. When you delete one of your Tweets it is also removed from your followers' Timelines.

Mentions

When a person's @username appears *anywhere* in a Tweet, this is known as a *mention*. Since replies always start off with @username, they can also be considered as mentions. If you click **Connect** on the Twitter menu bar and then select **Mentions**, the Tweets which contain your @username are listed.

In the example above, the two Tweets are mentions because they contain a username, **@StellaAustin7**. They are also replies because the username is at the beginning of the Tweet.

Favorites

If you like a Tweet, hover over it and click **Favorites**. This changes to **Favorited** (in gold) and a star appears in the top right-hand corner as shown below.

To undo a Favorite click **Favorited** as shown above. When you mark a Tweet as a Favorite, the person who posted the Tweet receives a notification in their **Interactions** tab under **Connect**.

Saving Favourite Tweets

Apart from telling someone you like their Tweet, marking as Favorites is a good way to save Tweets that you may want later. Your Favorited Tweets appear on your Profile page after clicking **Home**, **View my profile page** and then selecting **Favorites** in the left-hand panel.

Viewing Your Latest Tweets

You can view the Tweets (and Retweets) you have recently posted by clicking **Home**, **View my profile page** and then selecting **Tweets**, as shown below.

Hashtags

You often see in the middle of a Tweet, something like **#climate**. The hash sign (**#**) followed by a keyword such as **climate**, for example, is called a *hashtag*. The hashtag makes it very easy for you to find all the Tweets on popular topics. If you receive a Tweet containing a hashtag, clicking the hashtag displays all the Tweets involving that subject. You can create your own hashtags and you can type the name of an existing hashtag into the Twitter search bar. You could just type the keyword alone into the search bar but this produces a less precise search than the keyword. The hashtag search produces a list of Tweets which are specifically about the word or words in the hashtag.

Many organisations advertise their hashtag on their printed material or on TV. At the time of writing there is a big campaign to get a better deal for dairy farmers. Their posters prominently display the hashtag **#sosdairy**. Typing this into Twitter produces a huge list of Tweets specifically about the campaign.

Many of the Tweets found from the hashtag contain links to Web sites and documents containing much more information, such as photographs and scanned images.

Trends

These are topics which Twitter calculates are currently the most popular. Trends appear in a panel on the lower left-hand side of your Home page, as shown on the right. Clicking on any of the Trends as shown on the right displays a list of Tweets which relate to that topic. These appear on the right

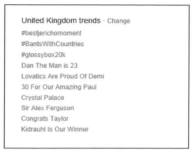

-hand panel of your Home page. As shown above, some Trends are also hashtags, as described on the previous page.

By default Twitter displays Worldwide Trends. This can be changed to show the Trends for a specific region by clicking the **Change** link shown at the top right above. In this example **United Kingdom/ London** has been selected, as shown below.

The button shown above, **Get tailored Trends** displays a list of trends based on your location and who you follow.

Posting a Photograph with a Tweet

A Tweet can be sent with a photograph of up to 3MB (megabytes) in size. Click the small, faint camera icon at the bottom left of the New Tweet window and then browse on your computer for the required photo. When you click **Open** a thumbnail of the image appears on the New Tweet window and the camera icon is now blue, as shown on the right.

After you click **Tweet** the message appears on your Timeline and on the Timelines of your followers as shown below.

The photograph appears as a link embedded in the Tweet. Click either the link **pic.twitter.com/HyWcHkpo** shown above or the link **View photo** to open the photo on the screen, together with the text of the message, as shown on the next page.

.

james gatenby
@jimgatenby

We photographed these two barn owl
chicks in a willow tree near our house
pic.twitter.com/OQnEAX2Y

← Reply   🗑 Delete   ★ Favorite

powered by 📷 Photobucket   Flag this media

3:49 AM - 22 Jul 12 via web ⋅ Embed this Tweet

Reply to @jimgatenby

Tweeting a Video

You can't post videos directly with a Tweet. However a video can
be posted to a video hosting Web site such as YouTube. Then
you can type the Web address of the video into a Tweet. This will
act as a link and a link enabling the video to be opened and
played from the host location. Including Web addresses in a
Tweet is discussed on the next page.

Posting a Web Link (URL) in a Tweet

You can use a Tweet to post a link to a Web site that you might want to share with someone else. Simply type the Web address (also known as a URL or Uniform Resource Locator) into the text of the message. In the example below, I entered the Web address **www.babanibooks.com** which Twitter shortened to babanibooks.com, as shown in blue below.

A Web address typed into a Tweet becomes a live link to the Web site. When someone receives a Tweet with a link, as shown above, clicking the link opens the Web site. On the bottom left of the Babani Web page is a link to the company's Twitter pages.

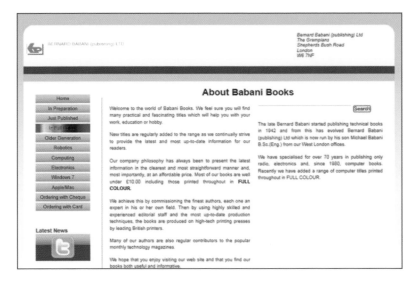

Including Your Location in a Tweet

This feature allows you to say where you are at the time of a Tweet and then include links to a map and photographs of the area. The *Location* feature is off by default but when you try to use it you are given the option to switch it on. When Location is switched on, its icon appears in blue at the bottom left of the New Tweet window, to the right of the camera icon, as shown on the right and in the screen extract below.

When you click the Location icon a search bar appears in which you enter and then select the required location. When you click the Tweet button, the message is posted, together with the link to your location (**from Entrevaux...**) shown in blue below, with the **Expand** option selected.

When your followers click the link **from Entrevaux...**, Google Maps opens up showing a map and photographs of the area.

Direct Messages

Two people can communicate by using the **Direct messages** option in Twitter. You send a direct message to one of your followers. This differs from the Tweet, which automatically goes to all of your followers, which may be a very large 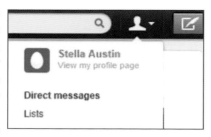 number in the case of a celebrity. Open the drop-down menu shown above on the right by clicking the person icon on the right of the Twitter menu bar and shown here on the right. Click **New Message** then enter the full name or username of your follower before entering the text of the message and clicking **Send Message**.

The recipient can read the message after clicking the person icon and selecting **Direct Messages** as shown above. Clicking the message opens a **Direct Message** window. This includes the original message and the sender's name, ready for the recipient to reply.

Sharing a Web Page Using a Tweet Link

Sometimes when you are surfing the Internet, you may see a Tweet button shown on the right. This can be used when you find a Web page you want to share with your followers. When you click the Tweet button or the bird icon, the following window opens with some text and a link to the Web page. Click the **Tweet** button shown on the lower right below.

The above Tweet is sent to all your followers' Timelines and to your own Timeline.

Your followers can click on the link **bbc.in/OiPHOf** to open the Web page which you wish to share with them.

Key Facts: Posting and Receiving Tweets

- A new Tweet can be up to 140 characters long and after posting appears on your Timeline and on the Timelines of the people following you.

- The full name and **@username** of the sender appear at the top of a Tweet. Clicking either opens their **Profile**.

- The **Reply** option on a Tweet appears when you click **Expand** or hover over a Tweet. Replies start off with the **@username** of the person posting the original Tweet.

- The **Retweet** button allows you to forward to your followers a Tweet received from someone else.

- You can also enter **RT@username** and type the text of the original message and any text of your own, to give credit to the original Tweeter.

- A **Hashtag** such as **#windfarms** in a Tweet is a link making it easy to find other Tweets on the same subject.

- Your **Mentions** are Tweets that have your username anywhere within them, so this includes replies to you.

- **Trends** are links to topics calculated by Twitter to be currently most popular, worldwide or in selected areas.

- You can post a photo in the form of a link in a Tweet. A recipient clicks the link to open the photograph.

- A Tweet can include a link to a Web page, typed or pasted in. The Web site is opened by clicking the link.

- A link in a Tweet can give your current **Location**. Clicking the link opens a map, photos and information.

- A **Direct message** is sent to just one of your followers.

- **Favorites** saves the Tweets you want to keep and tells the original Tweeter that you liked their Tweet.

- You can't **Edit** your Tweets but you can **Delete** them from your Timeline and from your followers' Timelines.

Personalizing Twitter

Introduction

When you first sign up for a Twitter account, you have the opportunity to enter some personal information, known as your Profile. It's not essential to complete your Profile during the sign up process. You can move on to start posting and receiving Tweets and finish your Profile later. For example, you might not have a suitable Profile photo immediately available. In this case Twitter inserts standard icons as shown on the right. These can be replaced with your own photo during the editing of your Profile and other settings which can be done at any time.

The following topics are described in this chapter:

- Changing your Account details.

- Changing your Twitter password.

- Making your Tweets Private, viewable only by approved followers.

- Editing your Profile, including adding a photograph and biographical information of less than 160 characters.

- Adding your mobile phone to your Twitter account.

- Controlling the e-mails sent to you by Twitter.

- Creating a background design for your Tweets and Profile.

- Checking the Apps (Applications) that can access your Twitter account.

Changing Your Account Details

Click the person icon on the right of the Twitter menu bar to open the drop-down menu shown on the right. Then select **Settings** to open the page below showing your Twitter **Account** details.

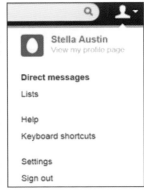

As shown in the extract below, you can change your **Username** by overtyping your old username, then entering your password and saving.

As discussed shortly, Twitter can send you e-mail notifications of activities on Twitter involving you. If you wish to use a different e-mail address, enter it in the **Email** bar shown below.

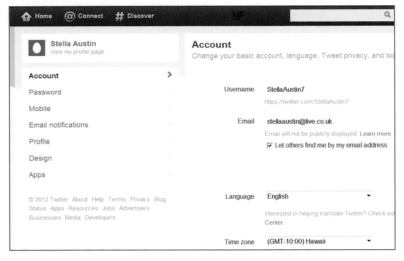

As shown in the extract above, there is an option to allow people to search for you on Twitter using your e-mail address. You can also change the **Language** and select a **Time zone**.

Tweet Privacy

Lower down the **Account** page shown on page 160, there is a check box, **Protect my Tweets**, as shown below.

Tweet privacy	☑ Protect my Tweets
	If selected, only those you approve will receive your Tweets. Your future Tweets will not be available publicly. Tweets posted previously may still be publicly visible in some places. **Learn more**

When you first start using Twitter your posts are set at Public access by default. Your Tweets will be visible to anyone who can find you on Twitter after entering your name, username or e-mail address into the search bar at the top of the Twitter screen.

If the **Protect my Tweets** check box is ticked, as shown above, your future Tweets will only be seen by your approved followers. If someone who is not an approved follower finds your account, they will need to click the **Follow** button and obtain your consent to become an approved follower.

Finally click **Save changes** at the bottom of the **Account** page.

Changing Your Twitter Password

Click **Password** on the left-hand panel of the **Settings** window shown on the previous page. Then enter your new password and verify it by retyping before clicking the **Save** changes button.

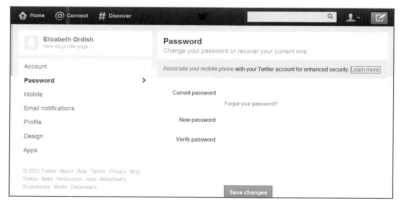

Editing Your Profile

From your Home page, click **View my profile page** and then click the **Edit your profile** button. Alternatively click the person icon, then **Settings** and **Profile**, as described on page 160.

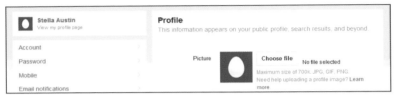

After clicking **Choose file** shown above you then browse your computer for the required photo as shown below. This might be stored on your hard disc drive or on a removable device such as flash drive. Browsing your computer for a photo was also discussed on pages 79 and 80 in the notes on Facebook.

Click **Open** to upload the picture to Twitter. After you click **Save changes** the picture appears on your Profile page as shown on the next page.

700K Twitter Profile Photo Size Limit

Please note that there is a 700K (kilobyte) size limit on Twitter Profile photos. So you might have to take a new photograph with a digital camera set on a low resolution setting. An existing photograph can be reduced to a lower file size by using programs such as Windows Live Photo Gallery or Adobe Photoshop Elements.

Make sure your full name is correctly entered in the **Name** slot above. If you want to, enter your **Location** and your **Website** address if you have one. Enter some biographical details in the box marked **Bio**, using less than 160 characters.

Click **Post your Tweets to Facebook** if you want them to appear on your Facebook Timeline/Wall. Finally click **Save changes** to complete the editing of your Profile page.

Working with photographs is covered in detail in our book Computing and Digital Photography for the Older Generation, ISBN 978-0-85934-729-7 from Bernard Babani (publishing) Ltd.

Your thumbnail picture appears at the top of your Profile page together with your biographical details as shown below. Your picture also appears on any Tweets that you post.

Stella Austin
@StellaAustin9
Former R-R secretary and bank employee now gardener, horse rider, cat lover and poultry keeper
Sutton on the Hill

If a lot of people have the same name as you, your thumbnail photograph will help people to find you on Twitter. After entering your name in the Twitter search bar and selecting **People** in the left-hand panel, your friends can look through the search results and recognise your photograph, as shown below.

When someone finds your entry in the list of results of a search, they can click your name and see your Profile and your Tweets. Your friends can also click the button to **Follow** you if they wish, as shown above.

Clicking **Email notifications** as shown on the Edit Profile extract on page 162 allows you to control whether Twitter sends you an e-mail after certain events have happened, as shown in the example below.

Mobile shown on the Edit Profile page allows you to set up your mobile phone and activate it to use Twitter. This includes downloading a Twitter mobile App or application (i.e. program) for smartphones such as the iPhone, Blackberry and those based on the Android and Windows Phone 7 operating systems.

Clicking **Apps** shown in the left-hand panel on page 163 displays which programs or Applications can access your Twitter account.

Changing the Background Design

The **Design** option on the Edit Profile page presents a large choice of colours and designs to use as a background to Twitter.

The design feature also allows you to upload images of your own to use in the background and these can be tiled if preferred.

Adding a Desktop Shortcut Icon for Twitter

Open the sign-in screen by entering **www.twitter.com**. Then right-click anywhere over the centre of the screen. From the menu that appears select **Create shortcut** and then click **Yes**.

You should now have a Twitter icon on your Windows Desktop which can be used in future to launch Twitter quickly by double-clicking the icon.

More Ways to Keep in Touch

Introduction

The previous chapters have described the most popular social networking Web sites, Facebook and Twitter, which each have hundreds of millions of users around the world. Facebook provides a platform for users to make *friends* with large numbers of users having similar interests and to share their latest news, photographs and videos. Twitter relies on people choosing to *follow* other people in whom they are interested and to read their latest thoughts, in the form of 140 character text messages or *Tweets*. These can include links to photographs and Web sites. Both Facebook and Twitter allow you to interact with large numbers of people — hundreds or even thousands.

Although Facebook and Twitter can be used for on-going conversations between a few close friends and family, many of the people who exchange information on these sites can be more accurately described as *contacts* rather than *close friends*.

This chapter looks at some other ways of communicating which may, on some occasions, be more suitable for close friends and family. The following applications are discussed:

- The *Blog* or Web log, i.e. an online diary.
- *E-mail* or *Electronic mail*.
- *Skype* and *Live Messenger* video telephone services.

Many people may find they use some or all of these applications at different times — Facebook, Twitter, Skype, Windows Live Messenger and e-mail depending on the situation.

The Blog

This is basically your own personal Web site. However, instead of creating Web pages from scratch in the HTML language, you just select the design of your blog from a set of ready-made templates. Simply type in the text and insert any pictures, as discussed shortly. Blogs are widely used by journalists and commentators as well as ordinary people who want to share ongoing events with friends and family. One of the most successful blogs, called NeverSeconds, was created by Martha Payne, a schoolgirl in Argyll, Scotland. This has attracted millions of followers and raised thousands of pounds for the children's charity Mary's Meals. Martha's blog features daily *posts* discussing each day's school meal, including photographs of the meals and comments from people around the world.

Like Martha's blog, some blogs are interactive, allowing other people to place replies and comments on the blogs. A blog can be kept by a single user or it can be the work of a team, group or a family — a *multiple author blog*. The text in a blog is generally more extensive than Twitter with its 140 character limit. Twitter is often referred to as a *microblog.* Like Twitter, the daily or regular posts in the blog are automatically marked with the date, with the latest posts placed at the top.

Setting up a blog is usually free and all you need to sign up and get started is a genuine e-mail address. When you set up your blog you are given a URL (Uniform Resource Locator) or Web address for the blog, as discussed on the next page. The address of your blog will be of the form:

yourname.blogspot.com

After you have given the *URL* to your friends and relatives they can type it into the address bar of their Web browser such as Internet Explorer. Alternatively you could send the URL as a live, clickable link in an e-mail or Tweet, as discussed elsewhere in this book. Or they could copy and paste the URL into their browser address bar or add your blog to your list of Favorites.

Creating a Blog

Blogger is a Web site provided by Google, Inc., which allows you to create a free blog. First log on to **www.blogger.com** and click **SIGN UP** to create a new Google account. You will then have a gmail address such as **jillsmith@gmail.com** and a password. These are used to sign in to Blogger. Next click the **New Blog** button to start creating your first blog, as shown below.

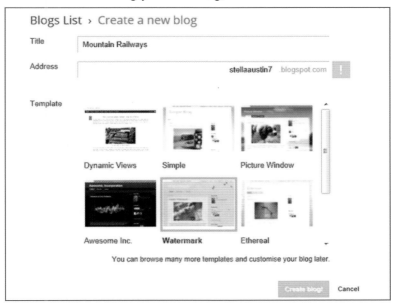

First enter a name for the blog, as in **Mountain Railways** above. Next in the **Address** bar enter your name, to precede **blogspot.com**, making the address of your blog something like:

stellaaustin7.blogspot.com

If your name has already been used by someone else, it can be modified by adding a digit such as in **stellaaustin7**.

As shown above there are several templates or designs to choose from, including **Watermark** chosen in this example and shown on page 171.

After choosing a template for the layout of the blog as discussed on the previous page, click the **Create Blog!** button to get started. Enter a name for the post, **Train des Pignes**, within the **Mountain Railways** blog, in this example. Now start typing in the text of the blog as shown below.

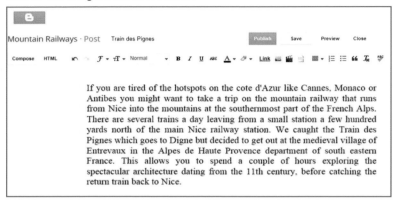

Unlike Twitter and Facebook, the blog has a wide range of formatting tools to control the size, style, colour and layout of the text, similar to a word processor or desktop publishing program.

Adding a Picture to a Blog

You can insert a picture into a post, after clicking the **Insert image** icon on the Toolbar as shown on the right and below. **Browse** to find the image on your computer then click **Add selected** to upload the picture to the blog.

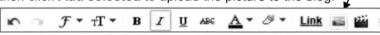

Browsing your computer's hard disc and various peripheral devices such as flash drives, camera cards and CDs/DVDs, etc., was covered in more detail in Chapters 2 and 7.

The **Link** button above allows you to insert in your post a hyperlink to a *Web page*. The icon shown on the right and above enables a *video* to be inserted in the post.

Previewing and Publishing a Blog

Click the **SAVE** button to save a draft of your blog. When you've finished entering the text and pictures, click **PREVIEW** to see what it will look like on the Web, as shown below.

The Blogger Web site lays out your post in the design template you selected when you created the blog. The post is automatically stamped with the current date.

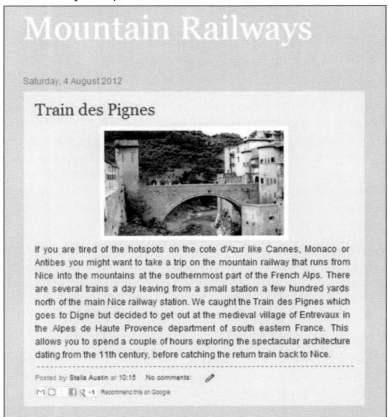

Finally click the **PUBLISH** button shown on the previous page to upload your latest post to your blog on the Blogger Web site.

Electronic Mail

E-mail can be thought of as an electronic version of the traditional letter, which it has replaced to a very large extent. Although perhaps not as fast a method of communication as Facebook, Twitter and instant messaging, it can be used for sending much more substantial messages and document files.

With e-mail you type a message, including any attachments consisting of photos, document, files or even video clips, then send it to one or more people from your list of contacts. Each of your e-mail contacts has a unique e-mail address of the type:

stellaaustin@live.co.uk

Outlook.com

At the time of writing Microsoft is launching a new e-mail service known as Outlook.com. This is a successor to the long standing service known as Hotmail, used by many millions of people around the world. With a new, cleaner user interface, Outlook.com is also designed to exchange updates with social networking sites like Facebook and Twitter. Users with existing Hotmail e-mail addresses can still use them with Outlook.com.

Web-based E-mail

E-mail services such as Outlook, Gmail (Google Mail) and Yahoo! Mail are *Web-based*, which means all your messages are stored on the Internet on the server computers of the service providers. You can access your Web mail easily from anywhere in the world, as long as you can connect to the Internet.

E-mail Attachments

These are files such as photos, documents, files and videos which can be "clipped" to an e-mail message and sent with it. Outlook.com gives access to Skydrive, the Microsoft "clouds" storage facility. Here you can save photos and other large files for other people to share, including Office documents such as Microsoft Word reports and Excel spreadsheets.

Creating an Outlook.com Account

An Outlook.com e-mail account is free to set up. Simply log on to **http://www.outlook.com**, click **Sign in** and enter a Hotmail or Windows Live ID, if you have one. If you haven't already got a Windows Live ID, click **Sign up** and create your own Windows Live username and password, such as **jeansmith@live.co.uk**. This will be used as your e-mail address for Outlook.com as well as giving access to other Windows Live services.

Receiving a Message

After signing up to Outlook.com is complete, your **Inbox** receives a welcome message from the Outlook Team, as shown below.

Click on the **Outlook Team** entry in the list of messages to view the full message, as shown below. An e-mail can also include clickable links or *hyperlinks* to connect to other Web sites.

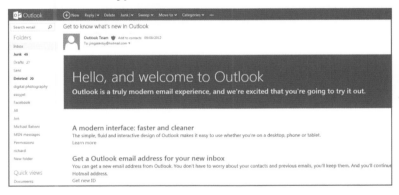

As shown on the left above, there are several ready-made folders such as **Junk** and **Deleted** and you can also create your own folders after clicking **New folder** in the left-hand panel. Across the top of the Inbox is the menu bar shown in the extract below, including options to start a **New** message.

After receiving a message you might **Delete** it, or store it in a folder using **Move to**. If you click **Reply** shown on the menu bar on the previous page, a blank space opens up at the top of the message ready for you to type in your reply. The e-mail address of the original sender is automatically inserted in the **To:** slot at the top of the message.

Michael Babani ×

Reply all on the menu bar on the previous page sends a copy of your reply to all the recipients of the original message. Clicking **Forward** allows you to send to other people a copy of a message you have received. Type their e-mail addresses into the **To** slot which appears and click **Send**.

Creating and Sending an E-mail

Click **New** as shown on the previous page and the following window opens. First enter the intended recipients' e-mail addresses in the **To:** bar shown above and below.

If you click **To** shown above you can select recipients from your address book or contacts list. Click **Cc** or **Bcc** on the right of the **To** bar to copy the e-mail to other recipients. Use *Carbon copies* (**Cc**) to keep other people informed. *Blind carbon copies* (**Bcc**) are sent covertly, i.e. without the other recipients knowing.

To see how an e-mail will be received, add your own address to the **To** list, send the message and then check your Inbox.

Now enter a title to replace **Add a subject**. As you can see below, the e-mail program has many text formatting features such as various fonts, bold, italics, coloured letters, etc. Start typing the new message in the blank right-hand panel.

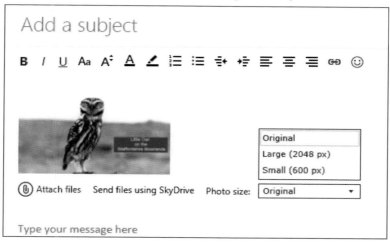

Including an Attachment

If you want to send a photo or document file with an e-mail, click **Attach files** shown above. Then browse your computer to find and attach the file. If you send files as attachments, the recipient clicks the name of the file to open it in its associated program, such as Windows Photo Viewer. As shown above you can also upload the files to **Skydrive**, so that other people can access them. Also shown above, Outlook.com has an option to reduce the size of a photo file in order to speed up sending over the Internet. Alternatively Windows Live Photo Gallery, part of Microsoft Windows Live Essentials, can be downloaded free and used to reduce the size of a photo to be uploaded to the Internet.

E-mail attachments are described in more detail in Computing and Digital Photography for the Older Generation from Bernard Babani (publishing) Ltd, ISBN 978-0-85934-729-7.

Free Worldwide Video Calls with Skype

Skype is a program which allows you to make phone calls over the Internet. The software can be downloaded free after typing the Skype address into your address bar, as shown below and then clicking the **Join Skype** button on the top right-hand side.

When using Skype calls between computers over the Internet are completely free, no matter where you are in the world. Each computer must have the Skype software and a microphone and speakers. Skype has a feature to test the microphone and speakers. The latest Skype software can be used with Windows XP, Windows Vista, Windows 7 and Windows 8.

Video

Skype allows both parties to call and see each other during a conversation, provided each machine is fitted with a webcam. Many new laptops and some tablet computers have the necessary speakers, microphone and webcam needed to run Skype. Otherwise you can buy removable plug-in versions of these devices which only cost a few pounds.

Making a Call

When you sign up to Skype, you need to create a unique name for yourself, rather than a telephone number. Skype is launched by clicking its icon on the Windows 7 Taskbar, as shown on the right and below.

When you start Skype, your contacts' names are listed down the left-hand side, as shown on the next page. The green icon with a tick shows that **Stellajill** is online to the Internet and can currently be called on Skype. This is confirmed by fact that the **Video call** button has a strong, not faint, green background.

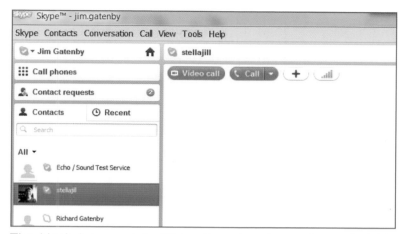

The blank icon next to Richard's entry above shows that his computer is not online to the Internet.

In this case the **Video call** button is very faint, meaning you cannot use Skype to call Richard's computer. You could, however, use Skype on your computer to call Richard's mobile phone or a landline. Calls from Skype to mobile phones and landlines require a Skype account with a credit balance.

Clicking **Echo/Sound Test Service** shown above and then **Call**, enables you to test your microphone as discussed previously.

Receiving a Call

When you receive a call you can click buttons to answer with or without video or decline the call, as shown below.

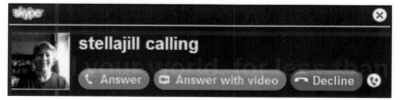

Windows Live Messenger

This is part of Microsoft Windows Live Essentials, a suite of Microsoft Windows additional programs. These can be downloaded free from the Web site **windows.microsoft.com** after selecting **Downloads** and **Windows Live Essentials**.

The program was originally known as MSN Messenger and was an IM (Instant Messaging) text messaging service. Now it allows free Internet phone calls with both voice and video in real time.

If you have downloaded and installed Windows Live Messenger, an icon should appear on the Windows 7 Taskbar, as shown on the right and below. Click this icon to launch Windows Live Messenger.

If you have an account with Hotmail or Outlook.com, your e-mail address is your Windows Live ID and can be used with your password to sign in to Windows Live Messenger.

After signing in you are given the chance to add friends from social networks such as Facebook. If any of your Messenger friends are currently online, their names appear in the top right-hand side of the screen, as shown in the case of **stella** below.

If you click the name of a friend who is online, the menu on the right opens. **IM** shown in the menu refers to an instant text message. **Start a video call** requires both computers to be fitted with webcams and microphones for the participants to see each other. Obviously the other person needs to be at the computer and ready to click the button to **Accept** the call as soon as dialing begins. If a friend does not answer a call you can leave them a video message. During a video call, the video of the

person you are calling appears large and can fill most of the screen. A thumbnail video of yourself appears at the bottom left of your own screen and large size on the screen of the person you are calling.

Windows Live Messenger allows you to share and discuss photographs with friends on screen, while chatting to them in a live video call. Messenger has been designed to integrate closely with Facebook, allowing Instant Messaging with Facebook friends. Messenger can also be used on the latest Windows and Android smartphones.

Like Skype, Messenger allows *free* video calls over the Internet between friends and family anywhere in the world.

Social Networking Tools at a Glance

The software and Web sites described in this book are each suitable for particular aspects of communication. They are all free and all allow sharing of photos, files and links to Web sites.

Facebook

Use this Web site to make friends with large numbers of like-minded people, with similar backgrounds and interests to yourself. Share latest news, photographs and events and display a Timeline showing how your life has evolved.

Twitter

Post off short, snappy "news flashes" and your current thoughts, join in hot debates and campaigns online and find out what celebrities and prominent people are saying. Hold text "conversations" in real time with friends and family.

Blogs

Keep an online Web diary for all to see, posting your own personal news or regular updates on an ongoing saga. Attractive Web pages, including photos and formatted text, are created easily using ready-made design templates.

E-mail

Send short or long formatted text messages to the e-mail addresses of one or more known contacts. E-mails can be much longer than posts using Facebook and Twitter. Photos, documents, files and video clips are sent as *attachments* or stored in the "clouds" for others to share.

Free Worldwide Telephone Calls Using the Internet

Speak free of charge to friends and family anywhere in the world and see them in live video, using Skype or Windows Live Messenger. Cheap calls from Skype to landlines and mobile phones are also available. Both Skype and Messsenger provide IM (Instant Messenging), the rapid exchange of text messages in a real time "chat".

Index